INTUITION OF THE INSTANT

Northwestern University
Studies in Phenomenology
and
Existential Philosophy

Founding Editor †James M. Edie

General Editor Anthony J. Steinbock

Associate Editor John McCumber

INTUITION OF THE INSTANT

Gaston Bachelard

Translated from the French by Eileen Rizo-Patron

Northwestern University Press
Evanston, Illinois

Northwestern University Press
www.nupress.northwestern.edu

10 9 8 7 6 5 4 3 2 1

Library of Congress Cataloging-in-Publication Data

Bachelard, Gaston, 1884–1962.
    [Intuition de l'instant. English]
    Intuition of the instant / Gaston Bachelard ; translated from the French by
Eileen Rizo-Patron.
       p. cm.—(Northwestern University studies in phenomenology and
existential philosophy)
    "Originally published in French in 1932 under the title L'intuition de
l'instant copyright (c) 1932, 1992, Editions Stock. Appendix B contains a
translated excerpt from *Introduction à la poétique de Bachelard*, by Jean Lescure,
copyright (c) 1966 by Editions Denoel."
    Includes bibliographical references and index.
    ISBN 978-0-8101-2904-7 (pbk. : alk. paper)
    ISBN 978-0-8101-2905-4 (cloth : alk. paper)
    1. Roupnel, Gaston, 1871–1946. Silöe. 2. Time perception. 3. Bachelard,
Gaston, 1884–1962. I. Lescure, Jean. II. Rizo-Patron, Eileen. III. Title.
IV. Series: Northwestern University studies in phenomenology & existential
philosophy.
B2430.R64B313 2013
153.753—dc23

2012036250

Contents

Translator's Preface

The last decades of twentieth-century philosophy witnessed a marked preoccupation with the discontinuous and the disruptive—whether in the form of epistemological and historical "cuts" (*coupures*) in Althusser, Canguilhem, and Foucault, the "differend" (Lyotard), the incursion of the symbolic (Lacan), or the trace in its differential power (Derrida). More recently, Jean-Luc Nancy explored the power of surprise in the upsurge of an event. This massive but multiform preoccupation is often regarded as a response to the formal continuities, homologies, and symmetries that were the object of structuralist linguistics and anthropology. Such an explanation, while true, overlooks the contribution of a figure who, though prominent in his own time, became eclipsed with the rise of the postmodern movement in the latter decades of the twentieth century. This is Gaston Bachelard (1884–1962), whose groundbreaking contributions to the philosophy of science, as well as to literary criticism and poetic theory, are today being rediscovered with burgeoning interest.

As early as 1928, in his *Essai sur la connaissance approchée,* Bachelard had shown that the discontinuous in the form of error and the unexpected, far from being an aberration or regression, was intrinsic to the progress of science. By 1932, with the publication of *L'intuition de l'instant,* Bachelard posited the instant as a shattering of the regnant Bergsonian model of sheer continuous duration. It also provided a positive model whereby human experience more generally could be understood in its nonassured, often unanticipated turns. By this tour de force, Bachelard was able to stake out a new style and direction in philosophical thought, one that would become increasingly fecund in the practical domains of literary criticism and the philosophy of science, as well as in fields related to psychology, neurobiology, and the creative and healing arts.[1]

Although *L'intuition de l'instant* (1932) was written during the epistemological period that launched Bachelard's career, it is remarkable that both recent French editions (Gonthier, 1966, and Stock, 1992) recognized it nonetheless as a "prelude" to Bachelard's work in philosophical poetics, judging by their inclusion of his subsequent essay "Instant poétique et instant métaphysique" (1939), as well as an extended *Introduction à la poétique de Bachelard* (Éditions Denoël, 1966) by poet Jean Lescure, who would soon become Bachelard's close disciple and friend.[2] The current English edition will endorse this admittedly unusual presentation of Bachelard's earliest essay on time—yet not without first laying out our reasons, and a few caveats, in these brief preliminary remarks.

The idea for *L'intuition de l'instant* alighted surprisingly as a response to an experimental philosophical drama, *Siloë* (1927), written by Gaston Roupnel, a modest friend and colleague from the University of Dijon, who ran a vineyard and shared Bachelard's deep love of the *champaignois* countryside.[3] Embedded in the conception of this poignant piece (a story of human and cosmic destiny woven together with elements of microbiology, physics, and metaphysics), Bachelard discovered an intrepid hypothesis on the nature of time that would help crystallize his own evolving epistemological ideas, and serve as a catalyst for his future work.

It is in order to highlight the sudden impact and recurring challenge of Bachelard's hermeneutics of *Siloë* vis-à-vis his oeuvre as a whole, that Jean Lescure would eventually propose a reverse-chronology reading of his teacher's lifework in his 1966 introduction to Bachelard—beginning with the posthumously published *Fragments d'une poétique du feu* (1988) and ending with *L'intuition de l'instant* (1932).[4] A provocative yet promising approach, given that Bachelard himself kept rethinking and reworking his early thesis in ever-expanding and unexpected contexts, as Lescure recounts, recalling their intimate conversations during the long years of their acquaintance. It was Lescure who back in 1938 had challenged Bachelard to contextualize his revolutionary thesis on temporality in terms of "poetic intuition" for the journal *Messages* he then directed—an invitation to which the philosopher of science readily responded with his 1939 article on the "poetic/metaphysical instant." From that point on, Bachelard began to turn his attention, with increasing conviction and intensity, to the powers of poetic language and reverie—starting with an analysis of Isidore Ducasse's *Chants de Maldoror* in *Lautréamont* (1939), followed by his book series on the elemental imagination (1938–48). One can indeed detect a spiral unfolding and gradual enrichment of Bachelard's ideas on temporality, poetics, and creative imagination—an astonishing coherence amid inner ruptures and tensions, best appreciated in its intricate interlacings as one shuttles back and forth between his earliest and his latest texts.

The reverse-chronology approach proposed by Lescure is, nonetheless, among several possible ways to read the works of Gaston Bachelard. It gives voice to one of the critical poles that emerged in the wake

of Bachelardian scholarship—another being the movement that reads
his oeuvre from the framework of his philosophy of objective knowledge. Cristina Chimisso for instance reads *L'intuition de l'instant* as a
book that furthers the scientific rationalism that Bachelard was deter-
mined to defend after his teacher Léon Brunschwig, countering some
of the trends of the Bergsonian movement then prevalent in French
philosophy.[5] *L'intuition de l'instant* is no doubt a product of Bachelard's earlier work on scientific epistemology—with its proposal of the
"epistemological breaks" necessary for the advancement of scientific
thought—broached here from the perspective of the thesis of discontinuous time that marked his departure from Henri Bergson. For further
epistemological elucidation of this Bachelardian text, English-speaking
readers may refer to two other particularly cogent studies of *L'intuition de
l'instant:* Mary McAllester's *Gaston Bachelard: Subversive Humanist* (University of Wisconsin Press, 1991), with its discussion of *L'intuition de l'instant*
as a synthesis of the philosopher's theory of knowledge as proposed in
his *Essai sur la connaissance approchée* (1928);[6] and Roch C. Smith's *Gaston
Bachelard* (Twayne, 1982), with its analysis of *L'intuition de l'instant* vis-
à-vis Bachelard's *Intuitions atomistiques* (1933). It is interesting that, while
reflecting on the author's epistemology and history of science (starting
with pre-Socratic thought), Roch Smith will also appeal to a nonchrono-
logical reading of Bachelard's oeuvre that presents *L'intuition de l'instant*
as heralding the impending aesthetic turn in Bachelard's philosophy.[7]

Alongside these interpretive approaches—or underlying both, al-
beit in distinct ways that merit future examination—*L'intuition de l'instant*
calls to be read as a propaedeutic to a moral metaphysics. Not only does
Bachelard clearly elicit such a reading in the concluding remarks of his
"Instant poétique et instant métaphysique," but close attention to the
argument in *L'intuition de l'instant* proper suggests that the approach de-
ployed in its chapters serves primarily as scaffolding that sets the stage for
an open-ended and more far-reaching philosophical undertaking. The
epistemological matrix that Bachelard had fine-tuned in earlier works,
such as *Essai sur la connaissance approchée,* prepared him to tackle analyti-
cally some of Roupnel's provocative insights in *Siloë,* a work whose roots
in the biological and microphysical sciences culminates in surprising
epiphanic breakthroughs, reminiscent of Dante's *Divine Comedy* though
written in lyrical prose. The combined rigor and candor of Bachelard's
reading of *Siloë*—which takes the ostensible shape of his polemic with
Bergson's thesis of temporal continuity and the élan vital[8]—thus breaks
open an unexpected path beyond itself. For the insight that strikes
Bachelard in Roupnel's book—an insight he comes to accept only after
examining a series of epistemological obstacles and evasions along the

way—is that of the brutal instant experienced when we are faced with the unexpected death of a loved one, or the sudden daunting realization of personal responsibility for the recurring errors and habits that rule over our thwarted lives or collective worldviews such as those that led to the two world wars in Bachelard's lifetime.[9] Only such a tragic realization may be capable of cutting deep into the heart of reason, referring us to Roupnel's suggestive title drawn from the fountain of Siloam in John's gospel (9:7–11)[10] as a power capable at a given moment—if we only heed and assent to it—of absolving the élan that otherwise seems to drive existence onward, relentlessly hauling the cumulative detritus of our past. This is what makes of Bachelard's first inquiry into the essence of time also a precursor to the "pedagogy of discontinuity" he will pursue throughout the rest of his career, starting with *La dialectique de la durée* (1936), and most explicitly developed in his *Philosophie du non* (1940).[11]

L'intuition de l'instant thus sets the stage for both an evolving "ethics of negation"—with its need to disrupt entrenched ideologies, epistemological constructs, habits or ill-made durations that so often drive human existence to fruitless impasses—and an "ethics of attention and welcome," a hermeneutics of sympathy most beautifully sung in Bachelard's "Preface to Buber's *I and Thou*" (1938),[12] as he focuses on the call of the "thou" in our fellow beings, as well as in the voices that emanate from the natural world, whose destiny is entrusted to our care.

It is Bachelard's sudden recognition of the profound ethical and religious dimensions of Roupnel's intuited instant—and of the dynamic fissure open(ing) at the heart of his scientific rationalism even as he composes his first piece on time—that reaffirms the value of appending a key excerpt from Jean Lescure's introduction to this translation of *L'intuition de l'instant*. For no one better than a close colleague and friend can offer firsthand testimony of Bachelard's remarkable combination of audacity, agility of mind, and humility in the face of mystery.

In the years following the Second World War, an urgent philosophical reflection on time's moral appeal would be significantly furthered by Emmanuel Levinas from sociopolitical perspectives that Bachelard himself had refrained from developing in an explicit way, given his confessed insufficiency in the disciplines of political philosophy and the social sciences. Levinas, who soon became a member of intellectual circles founded by Bachelard's colleague Jean Wahl in the late 1930s and 1940s, opted to focus specifically on the "ethical instant" in conferences delivered at the Philosophical College in 1946/47, later published as *Le temps et l'autre* (1948). In its precursor text, *De l'existence à l'existant* (1947), Levinas rejected the classical, abstract, representational idea of the instant, conceiving it instead as "the very accomplishment of existence" (76)—a notion that reopened the question of *l'instant fécond* proposed earlier in Bachelard's *L'intuition de l'instant* (1932). The potential convergences and divergences between Bachelard's and Levinas's thoughts on the ethical implications of the instant—not to mention their resonance with the idea of the "Messianic instant" (*Jetztzeit*) that Walter Benjamin had been pursuing, of his own accord, in the early decades of the twentieth century[13]—remain to be further explored and developed in continental philosophy.

Before closing these preliminary remarks, a few comments on technical aspects of this translation are in order. First of all, the 1992 Stock edition of *L'intuition de l'instant,* used as a main template for this translation, omitted a few lines from chapter 1, section 3—an omission that unfortunately interfered with the clarity of Bachelard's argument. This translated version restores that missing passage to reflect the original 1932 edition (as explained in note 10 to chapter 1 of Bachelard's text).

Second, some of the English terms used to render Bachelard's guiding concepts in this translation require foregrounding. For words that connote the negation of being, we have maintained key distinctions evident in the French. For instance, *le néant* is translated as "nothingness," whereas Bachelard's more specific *un néant* is rendered as "a void." The French *rien* appears as "nothing," and *vide* as "vacuum" (noun) or "empty" (adjective). Depending on context, certain cognates have been retained, such as the English "actual" for the French *actuel,* because Bachelard (after Roupnel) repeatedly emphasizes the "act" implied in whatever takes on concrete existence in the world of perceptual experience—unlike those potential events that remain lingering in a virtual state as unrealized appeals or possibilities whose moment has not yet come. The French term *esprit* is generally translated as "mind"—except in those instances where it clearly alludes to a spiritual dimension of experience, in which case the cognate "spirit" has been kept.

Third, Bachelard cites Samuel Butler's *Life and Habit* (1910) as one of his critical sources, yet he draws his references from Valéry Larbaud's French translation *La vie et l'habitude.* Bachelard's remarks in one or two instances respond to a figurative element in the French translation that had remained only implicit in Butler's original text. In such cases (noted in the text), we have found it necessary to retranslate the French version back into English, to retain the nuances highlighted in Bachelard's philosophical commentary.

While Bachelard retains Roupnel's old style of capitalizing key concepts in *L'intuition de l'instant* (1932)—for example, *Instant, Destin, Durée, Temps, Éternité, Art, Raison, Cosmos, Matière, Univers, Harmonie, Monde*—he discontinues this practice in his second volume on time, *La dialectique de la durée* (1936) as well as in his short essay "Instant poétique et instant métaphysique" (1939), where common nouns all appear in lowercase. The more modern usage has been kept in this translation, except in passages directly cited from Roupnel's *Siloë*, or in cases where the tenor of discourse manifestly rises to a hallowed register.

Lastly, all of Bachelard's notes to the text have been retained, verbatim, throughout this work, and are reproduced in the endnotes. Contextual and background references added by the translator for the English-speaking reader in continental philosophy also appear in the endnotes, distinguished by square brackets.

Notes

1. See for instance, Michèle Pichon's *Gaston Bachelard: L'intuition de l'instant au risque des neurosciences* (L'Harmattan, 2012), and the correlations she draws with neurologist Oliver Sacks's findings in *The Man Who Mistook His Wife for a Hat* (1987) and *Musicophilia* (2008). See also suggestions for further reading below.

2. Jean Wahl introduced Lescure to Bachelard in September 1938, after he had read *La dialectique de la durée* (1936). Years later, Bachelard would cite Lescure's poetry in several of his works on imagination: *L'air et les songes* (1943; *Air and Dreams*), *La terre et les reveries de la volonté* (1947; *Earth and Reveries of Will*), and *La poétique de l'espace* (1957; *Poetics of Space*).

3. The story of this friendship is recounted at length in Jean Lescure's *Un été avec Bachelard* (109–126). See suggestions for further reading.

4. Here we limit ourselves to summarizing Lescure's hermeneutic wager in his "Introduction à la poétique de Bachelard" (*L'intuition de l'instant*, 121ff.). An excerpt from the final sections of his piece (137–49) is reproduced as an addendum to this text, with permission of Éditions Denoël (1966).

5. See Cristina Chimisso's *Gaston Bachelard: Critic of Science and the Imagination* (120–24). London and New York: Routledge, 2001.

6. Another remarkable study by Mary McAllester, in this regard, is "The Redemptive Instant: Bachelard on the Epistemological and Existential Value of Surprise" (*Philosophy Today* 47, no. 5 [2003]: 124–31).

7. R. C. Smith tackles the link between Bachelard's scientific epistemology and his poetics in his earlier piece "Gaston Bachelard and the Power of Poetic Being" (*French Literary Review* 4 [1977]: 235–38.)

8. When Bachelard deconstructs Bergson by writing of "the *élan* furnished by the radical newness of *instants*," writes Casey, "we cannot help hearing . . . the

insistence that instants are the privileged, perhaps exclusive, vehicles of the new in its sheer otherness as well as in its being the same as ever-different" ("The Difference an Instant Makes," *Philosophy Today* 47, no. 5 [2003]: 122). Casey also finds in this essay a correlation between Bachelard's notion of the instant and Husserl's "source-point [*Quellepunkt*]," as both "originary [*ursprünglich*]" and "creative [*schöpferisch*]" (119).

9. Rooted upon a meditation on tragic death and the time of disaster, Bachelard's project of a philosophy of "repose" to be lived within intentional time developed, according to Perraudin, amid constant risk (see "Lire Bachelard avec Jean Lescure," in *Association des Amis de Gaston Bachelard*, bulletin no. 8 [2006]: 43).

10. The gravity of this religious dimension, which is kept at best latent throughout Bachelard's work, is probed in R. Kearney's "Bachelard and the Epiphanic Instant" (*Philosophy Today* 52 [2008]: 42–43). For a sounding of the sacred in Bachelard's poetic phenomenology, see also my "Awakening the Inner Ear: Gadamer and Bachelard in Search of a Living Logos," in *Translation and Literary Studies*, edited by M. Feltrin-Morris, D. Folaron, M.C. Guzmán, 57–67 (Manchester: St. Jerome's Press, 2012).

11. Bachelard's "pedagogy of discontinuity" can be traced, as well, in the conclusions to *Psychoanalysis of Fire* (1938), *Lautréamont* (1939), and further yet in Bachelard's psychological exploration of "culture complexes" in his books on the elemental imagination (1942–48; see complete list of Bachelard's works at the end of this work). Such pedagogy might be described as Bachelard's therapeutic quest for the sake of healing, but also as a condition for the possibility of "progress" in both the human and objective sciences. The question of progress launched in *L'intuition de l'instant* is critically explored in the context of Shelley's *Prometheus Unbound* in my essay "Bachelard's Subversive Hermeneutics" (*Religion and the Arts* 10, no. 3 [2006]: 355–73).

12. In his preface to Buber's "*I and Thou*," Bachelard fleshed out the significance of the "instant of the human person" alluded to in the conclusion to his "Instant poétique et instant métaphysique" (1939). Capturing the synergy between those two short pieces and *L'intuition de l'instant* (1932), Kearney offers an illuminating account of the "ethics of the instant" that underlies Bachelard's poetics, in his "Bachelard and the Epiphanic Instant" (41, 43–44).

13. See R. Kearney's intriguing note on Benjamin's "Messianic instant" (described as "dialectics at a standstill") vis-à-vis Bachelard's *instant fécond* ("Bachelard and the Epiphanic Instant," 45n18).

Suggestions for Further Reading

Benfey, Christopher, and Karen Remmler. *Artists, Intellectuals, and World War II.* Boston: University of Massachusetts Press, 2006.
Casey, Edward S. "The Difference an Instant Makes: Bachelard's Brilliant Breakthrough." *Philosophy Today* 47, no. 5 (2003): 118–23.

Chimisso, Cristina. *Gaston Bachelard: Critic of Science and the Imagination*. London: Routledge, 2001.

———. "Introduction, *The Dialectic of Duration* by Gaston Bachelard," 1–15. Manchester, Eng.: Clinamen, 2000.

Durie, Robin, ed. *Time & the Instant: Essays in the Physics and Philosophy of Time*. Manchester, Eng.: Clinamen, 2000.

Kearney, Richard. "Bachelard's Epiphanic Instant." *Philosophy Today* 52 (2008): 38–45.

Lescure, Jean. *Introduction à la poétique de Bachelard*. Paris: Éditions Denoël, 1966. In *L'Intuition de l'instant*, 115–49. Paris: Éditions Stock, 1992.

———. "Souvenir de Bachelard." In *Bachelard: Colloque de Cerisy*, 226–40. Paris: Union Générale d'Éditions, 1974.

———. *Un été avec Bachelard*. Paris: Luneau-Ascot Éditeurs, 1983.

Levinas, Emmanuel. *De l'existence à l'existant* (1947). Paris: J. Vrin, 1978.

———. *Le temps et l'autre* (1947). St. Clement, Fr.: Fata Morgana, 1979. Eng. trans. *Time and the Other*, trans. Richard Cohen. Pittsburgh, PA: Duquesne University Press, 1987.

McAllester Jones, Mary. *Gaston Bachelard: Subversive Humanist*. Madison: University of Wisconsin Press, 1991.

———. "The Redemptive Instant: Bachelard on the Epistemological and Existential Value of Surprise." *Philosophy Today* 47, no. 5 (2003): 124–31.

Perraudin, Jean-François. "Lire Bachelard avec Jean Lescure." In *Association des Amis de Gaston Bachelard*, bulletin no. 8 (2006): 41–57.

———. "Un Bachelard non-bergsonien." In *Gaston Bachelard: Du rêveur ironiste au pédagogue inspiré*, ed. Jean Libis, 61–76. Dijon : C.R.D.P., 1984. Eng. trans. "A Non-Bergsonian Bachelard," trans. Eileen Rizo-Patron. *Continental Philososphy Review* 41 (2008): 463–79.

Pichon, Michèle. *Gaston Bachelard: L'intuition de l'instant au risque des neurosciences*. Paris: L'Harmattan, 2012.

Préclaire, Madeleine. "Vers *Siloë*." In *Une poétique de l'homme: Essai sur l'imagination d'après l'oeuvre de Gaston Bachelard*, 89–156. Montréal: Éditions Bellarmin, 1971.

Rizo-Patron, Eileen. "Awakening the Inner Ear: Gadamer and Bachelard in Search of a Living Logos." In *Translation and Literary Studies*. Manchester, Eng.: St. Jerome, 2012.

———. "Bachelard's Subversive Hermeneutics." *Religion and the Arts* 10, no. 3 (2006): 355–73.

Roupnel, Gaston. *Siloë*. Paris: Librairie Stock, 1927.

Smith, Roch C. *Gaston Bachelard*. Boston: Twayne, 1982.

———. "Gaston Bachelard and the Poetic Power of Being." In *Twentieth-Century Literary Criticism*, vol. 128, pp. 44–46. Detroit: Gale Research, 2003.

Acknowledgments

This translated edition of Bachelard's *L'intuition de l'instant* was made possible thanks to the encouragement of Edward S. Casey and Richard Kearney who, on reading the initial draft, recommended the manuscript be submitted for publication to Northwestern University Press.

I would especially like to acknowledge the contribution of three French scholars, colleagues, and friends, each of whom left a bright mark on this Bachelard translation project. My gratitude goes first of all to Marilyn Gaddis-Rose, founder of the doctoral program in translation studies at Binghamton University, for her expert guidance at the early stages of composing this manuscript; to Edward K. Kaplan, Bachelard scholar and Baudelaire translator from Brandeis University, for his close reading and insightful suggestions mid-stage through the project; and to Roch C. Smith, emeritus professor of French literature at the University of North Carolina, Greensboro, for his rereading of the complete manuscript against the French original and helpful comments at its final revision stage.

The editors and editorial assistants at Northwestern University Press—Anthony Steinbock, Jane F. Bunker, Henry L. Carrigan Jr., Anne Gendler, Gianna Mosser, and Paul Mendelson—deserve my deep appreciation for their valuable support and assistance at various stages in the production of this text, as does my sister Jane Rizo-Patron, for her avid interest in listening to me read and discuss with her key passages from Bachelard's work over the phone.

I dedicate this translation to the memory of my father, Alfonso Rizo-Patrón Remy (1917–2012), who launched me in the exploration of the poetic interface between religion and science, and who taught my family the sacred value of every moment by reminding us, time and again, that "life is an instant poised between two eternities."

INTUITION OF THE INSTANT

Introduction

pren how all

When a ~~cultured and sensitive~~ soul retraces its efforts to lay down the great lineaments of reason according to its own intellectual destiny, when it retraces the history of its own culture through memory, it becomes aware that the vestige of an essential ignorance lies forever at the core of its intimate certainties. Within the realm of knowledge itself, there is indeed an original fault—that of having an origin; that of falling short of the glory of atemporal being; that of not awakening oneself to remain oneself, but of awaiting the lesson of light from the dark world.

In what glistening waters shall we find not only the renewal of rational freshness, but also the right to the eternal return of the act of reason? What Siloam, marking us with the sign of pure reason, will bring enough order into our mind and spirit to allow us to understand the supreme order of things? What divine grace will grant us the power to harmonize the beginnings of being and the beginnings of thought, and—by truly inaugurating us in a novel thought—to take up again the Creator's task within us, for us, and through our own minds? It is this fountain of intellectual youth that Roupnel seeks, as a good diviner, within all the domains of mind and heart. As we follow him—ourselves quite awkward at handling the forked branch of the hazel tree—we will perhaps fail to recover all the living waters or to sense all the subterranean currents of such a profound work. But at least we hope to convey at which points of *Siloë* we have received the most powerful and effective impetus, and which novel themes Roupnel offers the philosopher who seeks to meditate upon the problems of duration and the instant, of habit and life.

This work contains, first of all, a secret hearth. We do not know the source of its light and heat. Nor can we determine the exact moment when the mystery became clear enough to announce itself as a burning question. But no matter! Whether it comes from suffering, or whether it comes from joy, we all experience as human beings this moment of illumination at some point in our lives: a moment when we suddenly understand our own message, a moment when knowledge, by shedding light on passion, detects at once the rules and relentlessness of destiny—a truly synthetic moment when decisive failure, by rendering us conscious of the irrational, becomes the success of thought. That is the locus of the differential of knowledge, the Newtonian burst that allows us to ap-

3

preciate how insight springs forth from ignorance—the sudden inflection of human genius upon the curvature of life's progress. Intellectual courage consists in actively and vitally preserving this instant of nascent knowledge, of making it the unceasing fountain of our intuition, and of designing, with the subjective history of our errors and faults, the model of a better, more illumined life. The cohering value of the hidden, yet persistent, action of such a philosophical intuition can be felt traversing Roupnel's book. Even if the author does not reveal the primary source of his intuition, one can make no mistake about its unity and depth. The lyricism guiding this philosophical drama, *Siloë*, is the sign of its intimacy, for, as Renan once wrote, "what we say of ourselves is always poetry."[1] Because of its complete spontaneity, this lyricism carries a power of persuasion that we will probably fail to convey through this study. One would have to relive the entire book, following it line by line, to understand how much its aesthetic character adds to its clarity. To read *Siloë* well one must further realize that it is the work of a poet, a psychologist, and a historian who resists being a philosopher even at the very moment when his solitary meditation grants him the most beautiful of philosophical rewards, that of turning both soul and mind toward an original intuition.

Our main task in the essay that follows will be to bring this new intuition to light, and to show its metaphysical interest.

Before we embark on this exploration, however, some preliminary remarks may be useful to justify our method of choice.

Our aim is not to summarize Roupnel's book. *Siloë* is a book rich in thought and facts. Rather than summarized, it needs to be developed. While Roupnel's novels are animated by genuine verbal joy, by the prolific life of words and rhythms, it is remarkable that in *Siloë* he happens to strike upon the pithy phrase, fully gathered at the hearth of intuition. In this case, to explain entails unfolding what lies implicit in the text. We have therefore taken the intuitions of *Siloë* back as close as possible to their source, as we strive to heed the promptings these intuitions could provide to philosophical meditation. For several months, they have become the setting and framework of our deliberations. After all, an intuition is experienced, not proven. And it is experienced by multiplying, or even modifying, the conditions of its use. As Samuel Butler rightly noted: "If a truth is not sturdy enough to endure distortion and rough handling, it does not belong to a very robust species."[2] Indeed, it is through the very deformations to which we have subjected Roupnel's theses that readers may be able to measure their true force. We have thus made free use of the intuitions of *Siloë* and—in a final analysis—more than an objective account, what we offer here is our experience of the book.

If, however, the integrity of Roupnel's text is much too deformed by our arabesques, readers may always restore its unity by returning to the mysterious source of the work. As we will attempt to show below, the same key intuition keeps reemerging in this book. Roupnel tells us, moreover, that its strange title is truly intelligible only to himself (*Siloë*, 8). Is this not also a way of inviting his readers to bring their own Siloam, the mysterious refuge of their own personality, to bear upon their reading? Each reader thus receives from the work a strangely moving and personal lesson that confirms its unity on a new level. In a word: *Siloë is a lesson in solitude.* This is why its intimacy is so deep; this is why it is sure to keep the unity of its intimate force notwithstanding the scattered unfolding of its chapters, and despite our overextensive commentaries.

Let us now focus on the guiding intuitions of *Siloë* without forcing ourselves to follow the order of the book. It is these intuitions that will provide the most helpful keys to open up the multiple perspectives on which the work unfolds.

1

The Instant

Lively, lovely, virginal today.
—Stéphane Mallarmé, "Plusieurs sonnets," 1885

We shall not even know that we have met.
Yet meet we shall, and then part and meet again,
Where dead men meet, on lips of living men.
—Samuel Butler, Sonnet XIV, "Life After Death," 1918

I

The decisive metaphysical proposition in Roupnel's book is this: *Time has but one reality, the reality of the instant.* Otherwise put, time is a reality confined to the instant and suspended between two voids. Although time will no doubt be reborn, it must first die. It cannot transport its being from one instant to another in order to forge a duration. The instant is already solitude . . . It is solitude in its barest metaphysical value. Yet an even more poignant solitude confirms the tragic solitude of the instant: through a sort of creative violence, time limited to the instant isolates us not only from others but even from ourselves, since it breaks with our most cherished past.

Thus, from the very threshold of his meditation—and meditation on time is the preliminary task of every metaphysics—the philosopher asserts the idea that time presents itself as the solitary instant, as the consciousness of solitude. Later on, we will see how the phantom of the past or the illusion of the future will come to be reconstituted. Yet above all, to reach a full understanding of Roupnel's *Siloë,* we must first become

Stéphane Mallarmé, "Plusieurs sonnets." In *Oeuvres complètes,* edited by Henri Mondor and G. Jean-Aubry (Paris: Gallimard Pleiade, 1945), p. 67. First published in *La Revue Indépendante* (March 1885), and reprinted with no change in *Poésies* (1887).

steeped in the total equivalence of the present instant and what is real. How could the real escape the mark of the present instant? And, reciprocally, how could the present instant fail to make its mark on the real? If being is conscious of itself only in the present instant, how could we not realize that the present instant is the sole domain in which reality is experienced? If we were eventually to eliminate our being, we would still have to start from ourselves to prove being. So let us begin by observing our thought, and we will notice it fading away incessantly with each passing instant, without a memory of what has just taken leave of us, nor with any real anticipation or conscious grasp of what the coming instant will deliver. For "we are conscious of the present, and only of the present," claims Roupnel.

> The instant that has just fled from us is the same vast death that holds dominion over abolished worlds and extinguished firmaments. And the same fearsome unknown holds the approaching instant within the dark shadows of the future, as much as it does the Worlds and the Heavens that have yet no inkling of themselves.[1]

Roupnel moreover adds a claim that we shall presently counter with the sole purpose of accentuating his thought: "There are no degrees within this death, which is as much future as it is past." To reinforce the isolation of the instant even further, we would go as far as to say that there are degrees within death, and that what has just disappeared is deader than death itself . . . Meditation on the instant thus convinces us that oblivion is most brutal the more recent the past it destroys, just as uncertainty is most poignant when placed along the axis of a thought to come, of a still fervent yet already broken dream. A rather coherent and solid phantom might return from a more distant past, and live again through the effects of a purely formal permanence, which we will examine in due course. But the instant that just struck cannot be retained in its uniqueness as a complete being, for the recollection of many instants is necessary to create a complete memory. Likewise, the cruelest mourning is the awareness of a future betrayed. When that shattering instant arrives as the eyes of a cherished being close forever, we immediately feel the hostile novelty of the next instant that comes to pierce the heart.

It is this dramatic quality that perhaps best enables us to sense the reality of the instant. For it is, indeed, in the experience of a certain rupture of being that the idea of discontinuity imposes itself without dispute. Some might object that such dramatic instants separate two more monotonous durations. But we label "monotonous and regular" only those subtle developments we fail to examine with passionate attention.

If our heart were large enough to love life in all its details, we would see that every instant is at once a giver and a plunderer, and that a young or tragic novelty—always sudden—never ceases to illustrate the essential discontinuity of time.

II

This consecration of the instant as time's primordial element cannot be conclusive, however, unless and until the notion of the instant has first been confronted with the notion of duration. The reader cannot fail to be reminded of Bergson's theses, at this point, even though *Siloë* itself bears no trace of polemical thought. Since in this essay we have set ourselves the task of disclosing the thought processes of an attentive reader,[2] we must hence offer a step-by-step account of the objections arising from our recollection of Bergson's arguments. The intuition we are presenting here may indeed be best understood once we have set Roupnel's theory vis-à-vis Bergson's.

The plan of our discussion is as follows: First, we will recall the essential points of the theory of duration and develop the two terms of the opposition as clearly as possible: Bergson's philosophy as a philosophy of duration; Roupnel's philosophy as a philosophy of the instant. Next, we will spell out our tentative efforts at reconciling both theories; but we will not endorse this intermediary doctrine, which momentarily captured our attention. If we retrace it here, it is because it is bound to appeal to eclectic readers, deferring the need to take a stand. Following an account of our own debates, the reader will ultimately be able to appreciate why it is that, in our view, Roupnel's theory continues to be the clearest and most prudent position corresponding to the most direct consciousness of time.

So let us begin by reviewing Bergson's thesis. According to Bergson, we experience duration intimately and directly, as an immediate datum of consciousness. Such duration may of course be eventually developed, objectified, deformed. Committed to abstraction, for instance, physicists have developed a notion of uniform and lifeless time without limit or discontinuity. This entirely dehumanized time has then been handed over to mathematicians. Upon entering the domain of such prophets of the abstract, time is hence reduced to a simple algebraic variable—the variable par excellence—better suited to the analysis of the possible than to the examination of the real. Continuity is indeed a schema of pure possibility for mathematicians, rather than an essential character of reality. What then is the instant, in Bergson's view? It is no more than an artificial rupture that facilitates the schematic thinking of geometricians. The human intellect, in its ineptitude to pursue what is vital, immobilizes time within an ever-artificial present. Such present is pure nothingness— a nothingness that cannot even succeed at truly separating past from future. It seems indeed that the past carries its forces into the future, and that the future is necessary as an outlet for forces issuing from the past. A single sweeping life force, an identical élan vital, would thus suffice to consolidate duration. Thought, as a fragment of life, should not impose its rules upon life. Devoted as it is to the contemplation of static being, of spatial being, the intellect must guard against misunderstanding the reality of becoming. In the end, Bergsonian philosophy merges past and future indissolubly. It then becomes necessary for us to take time as a whole, if we are to grasp its reality. Time is at the very source of the élan vital. Though life may be showered with flashes of insight, it is truly duration that explains life.

Bergsonian intuition thus recapitulated, let us now consider some of the difficulties most likely to build up against it. We begin with a backlash against Bergson's critique of the reality of the instant.

If the instant is indeed no more than a false caesura, it will be very difficult for us to distinguish past and future, since their separation is purely artificial. We will then have to take duration as an indestructible unity. Hence all the consequences of Bergsonian philosophy—namely, that in each of our acts, in the least of our gestures, we should be able to grasp the completeness of what is just unfolding: the end in the beginning, being and all its becoming within the thrust [élan] of the seed.

But suppose past and future could be blended definitively. Within the terms of this hypothesis, one difficulty is likely to confront anyone willing to push Bergson's intuition to its limit. Having succeeded in proving the unreality of the instant, how then can we speak of the beginning of an act? What supernatural power, lying beyond duration, will enjoy the privilege of assigning a decisive role to a fertile moment which, if it is to endure, must yet begin? Such a doctrine of origins—the importance of which will become patent in Roupnel's philosophy—would be doomed to obscurity in a counter-philosophy that denies the value of instantaneity! Pondering life in midstream, in its growth, in its ascent, we could of course always show, with Bergson, that the words *before* and *after* serve merely as reference points, for between past and future an evolution can be traced that seems continuous by virtue of its general success. However, if we move into the domain of abrupt mutations, where the creative act takes place at one stroke, how could we fail to acknowledge that a new era always opens up through the irruption of an absolute? For every evolution—to the extent that it is decisive—is punctuated by creative instants.

As for knowledge of the creative instant itself, where is it most certainly attained if not in the experience of a sudden burst of consciousness? Isn't the élan vital most active in that instant, that sudden burst? Why attempt to return to some muted and buried power that has more or less lost its own thrust, unable to realize it fully or even to continue it, when we can witness before our very eyes, in the active present, the myriad accidents of our own cultural growth, the countless attempts to renew and to create ourselves? So let us return to the starting point of idealism, and take our own mind, in its efforts toward knowledge, as our field of experimentation. Knowledge is preeminently the work of time. Let us try, then, to release the mind from the bonds of flesh, from material prisons. As soon as it is set free, and to the degree that it is free, we will realize that the mind is the receptor of a myriad incidents, that the course of its reverie is smashed into a myriad segments suspended from immeasurable heights. In its labor of knowledge, the mind manifests itself as a series of discrete instants. It is in writing the history of knowledge that the psychologist, like every historian, artificially introduces the string of duration. Deep within ourselves, where the feeling of gratuitousness is so clear, we cannot grasp the causal force that would impel duration. Hence the question of seeking causes within a mind where only ideas can be born is at best but a sideline, an academic problem.

To summarize, whatever our assessment of duration itself, understood in terms of Bergsonian intuition (which we do not claim to have put on trial in these few pages), we must now at least admit the decisive reality of the instant, alongside duration.

To be sure, the opportunity will come to resume our debate against the theory of duration as an *immediate datum* of consciousness. Deploying Roupnel's intuitions toward that end, we intend to show how duration can be forged with instants that have no duration. This, we believe, will provide proof positive of the instant's primordial metaphysical character and, hence, of the indirect and mediate nature of duration.

At this point, however, we are eager to return to our constructive discussion. In view of the fact that Bergson's method encourages us to make use of psychological observation, we must concur with Roupnel that

> the Idea we have of the present is distinctively plentiful and teeming
> with positive evidence. We inhabit the present with our entire personal-

ity. It is in virtue of this present alone—in it and through it—that we become aware of existence. There is an absolute identity between the feeling of the present and the feeling of life. (*Siloë*, 108)

From the standpoint of life itself, we must therefore attempt to understand the past through the present, which is far different from striving ceaselessly to explain the present through the past. Eventually, no doubt, the feeling of duration must be elucidated. But for the time being let us simply take it as a fact: duration is a sensation like any other, as complex as any other. And let us not recoil from underlining its apparently contradictory character: duration is made up of durationless instants, just as a straight line is made up of dimensionless points. In order for entities to contradict each other, they must first of all interact within the same zone or realm of being. But if we establish that duration is a relative and secondary datum, always more or less artificial, how could our illusion of it contradict our immediate experience of the *instant*? All these reservations are here expressed so that we may not be accused of stumbling into a formal vicious circle, when we are in fact taking the words "duration" and "instant" in their ordinary sense, without adhering to their technical meaning. Granting these caveats, we can say with Roupnel:

> Our acts of attention are extraordinary episodes extracted from that continuity called duration. But the continuous fabric where our mind embroiders the discontinuous designs of acts is itself no more than the laborious and artificial construct of our mind. Nothing entitles us to posit objective duration. Everything in us contradicts its meaning, and undercuts its logic. Our instinct is indeed better informed about this matter than is our reason. The feeling we get of the past is one of negation and destruction. The credit our mind grants to an alleged duration that is no longer, where it can no longer be, is insufficient. (*Siloë*, 109)

In this passage we must underscore the role of the act of attention in the experience of the *instant*. For there is no real evidence of such an experience other than in an act of will, in the consciousness that intensifies itself to the point it decides to act.

The action that unfolds after the act already falls within the scope of logically and physically passive consequences. And this is a subtle but important detail that sets Roupnel's philosophy apart from Bergson's: *Bergsonian philosophy is a philosophy of action; Roupnelian philosophy is a philosophy of the act.* For Bergson, an action is always a continuous development that posits an underlying duration between a decision and its goal (each more or less schematic)—a duration that is always original and real. For a Roupnel supporter, an act is above all an instantaneous decision, and it is this decision that bears all the charge of originality. To speak in more physical terms, the fact that a mechanical impulse presents itself always as a composition of two infinitesimally different orders leads us to reduce the decisive and shocking instant down to its punctual limit. A percussive blow, for instance, could be explained as an infinitely great force that develops within an infinitely short time. It would also be possible to trace the analysis of a decision's consequent unfolding in terms of subordinate decisions. We might then see that a varying movement—the only kind Bergson rightly deems real—continues by following the same principles that set it in motion in the first place. Yet, as the action following the founding act is entrusted to less and less conscious organic reflexes, the discontinuities in its sequential development become increasingly difficult to observe. That is why we must return to clear acts of consciousness in order to detect the instant.

When we reach the final pages of this essay, we will need to return to this *actual* and *active* notion of the experience of the instant, in order to understand the relationship between time and progress. We will then realize that life cannot be understood in passive contemplation. Understanding life is more than just living it; it is indeed propelling it forward. Life does not flow along a slope on the axis of objective time that would serve as its channel. Although it may be a form imposed upon time's successive instants, life always finds its primary reality in an instant. Hence, if we delve into the heart of psychological evidence, to the point where sensation is no more than the complex reflection or response of a simple act of volition—when intense attention concentrates life's focus upon a single isolated element—then we will become aware that the instant is the truly specific character of time. The more deeply penetrating our meditation on time, the more minute it becomes. Idleness alone lingers; the act is instantaneous. Could we not say then, conversely, that instantaneity is an act? Take a weak idea, tighten its focus upon an instant, and it will suddenly illumine the mind. Being's repose, on the other hand, is already nothingness.

How could we therefore fail to see that the nature of the act is—quite literally—to be *actual*? And how could we then fail to realize that life is the discontinuity of acts? It is this intuition that Roupnel presents with particular clarity to us:

> It has been said that duration is life. Surely. But life should at least
> be placed within the frame of *discontinuity* that contains it, and in the
> pulsating form that manifests it.[3] It is no longer that fluid continuity
> of organic phenomena seen as flowing into one another and fusing
> in functional unity. Being, that strange site of material memories, is to
> itself but a habit. Whatever permanence there may be within being is

the expression not of an immutable and constant cause but rather of
a juxtaposition of effects, both fleeting and unceasing, each of which
has its own solitary source, yet whose binding tie—itself no more than a
habit—molds an individual. (*Siloë,* 109)

When composing his epic of evolution, Bergson no doubt had to
disregard accidents. Roupnel on the other hand, as a meticulous historian, could not ignore the fact that each act, no matter how simple,
necessarily breaks the continuity of vital becoming. If we examine the
history of life in detail, we will soon realize that it is a history like any
other—full of repetitions and anachronisms, full of trials, setbacks,
resumptions. Amid these accidents, Bergson retained only those revolutionary acts where the élan vital would split, where the genealogical
tree would branch out in different directions. To compose such a huge
fresco, he did not need to draw all the details. Indeed, rather than delineate objects, what he had to do was to produce the impressionist paint-
ing that became his magnum opus, *Creative Evolution* [*L'évolution créatrice,*
1907]—a vast illustrated intuition that is more the image of a soul than
it is a portrait of things.

But the philosopher who aims at describing the history of things,
of living beings, and of the mind—atom by atom, cell by cell, thought
by thought—must come to detach facts from one another. For facts, besides being facts, are acts. And acts, however unfinished or unsuccessful,
must necessarily *begin* in the absolute of a birth. Effective history must be
described via beginnings. Following Roupnel, we must create a doctrine
of *the accident as principle.*[1]

There is but one general law in truly creative evolution—the law
that an accident lies at the root of every evolutionary attempt.

Roupnel's temporal intuition thus appears to be the exact opposite of
Bergson's intuition, both in its consequences relative to the evolution
of life, as well as in its initial intuitive form. But before we proceed, let
us summarize the opposition between these two doctrines through a
double outline:

For Bergson, time's true reality is its duration. The instant is but
an abstraction devoid of reality. It is imposed from without by the intellect, which can understand becoming only by apprehending motionless states. Thus, Bergsonian time could be adequately represented by a
straight black line, with a white dot symbolizing the instant as a blank,
an imaginary void.

For Roupnel, time's true reality is the instant. Duration is but a
construction lacking any absolute reality. It is forged from without by

memory, that preeminent power of the imagination which seeks to dream and relive, but not to understand. Roupnelian time could thus be adequately represented by a straight white line—pure potentiality, pure possibility—where a black dot comes suddenly to inscribe itself as an unforeseeable accident, a symbol of opaque reality.

We must further note that this linear placement of instants remains—for Roupnel as for Bergson—an artifice of the imagination. Bergson finds an indirect means to measure time in this duration that unfolds in space. But length of time does not represent the value of a duration, and it would be necessary to retrace one's steps back from extensive time to intensive duration. Here again, the thesis of discontinuity can readily be adapted: intensity lends itself to being analyzed by the number of instants in which the will achieves clarity of purpose and sharpness of focus, just as easily as by the gradual and fluent enrichment of the self.[5]

Before we develop the perspective laid out in *Siloë* with greater precision, however, let us open a brief personal parenthesis.

III

We admitted earlier how long we had personally hesitated between the two aforementioned intuitions, even as we explored conciliatory ways to bring together under a single schema the advantages of each of these doctrines. Ultimately, we did not find satisfaction in that eclectic ideal. Nonetheless, since one of the tasks we took upon ourselves was to study our own intuitive reactions to the dominant idea just outlined, we now owe it to the reader to provide a detailed confession of our failure.

Initially, we would have liked to attribute a dimension to the instant, to make it a kind of temporal atom that would retain within itself a certain duration. We assumed that an isolated event should have a short logical history in reference to itself, within the absolute of its internal evolution. We understood well that its beginning could be relative to an accident of external origin. But for that brief event to shine, and later to decline and die, we demanded that its share of time—however isolated—be attributed to being. Although we took the fervent yet fleeting life of a mayfly as our model of life, from the dawn to the nuptial flight of this short-lived creature we also reclaimed its treasure of inner life. We still wanted duration to be a profound and immediate richness of being. That was indeed our first stance regarding the *instant*, which would have constituted a small fragment of Bergsonian continuity.

From Roupnelian time, this is what we then borrowed: We imagined that temporal atoms could not touch each other or, rather, that they could not merge into one another. What would always keep such fusion from taking place was the imprescriptible novelty of instants, of which the doctrine of accidents found in *Siloë* had convinced us. In a doctrine of substance, which is close indeed to being tautological, qualities and recollections may be readily transmitted from one instant to another. Yet permanence can never explain becoming. Thus, if novelty is essential to becoming, one has everything to gain by attributing such novelty to time itself: what is novel within uniform time is not being but the instant, which, in renewing itself, carries being back to its original freedom, to the initial accident or chance of becoming.

Besides, when it strikes, the instant imposes itself all in one blow, completely. It is the agent of being's synthesis. According to this theory, the instant then necessarily retains its individuality. As for the problem of knowing whether temporal atoms touch each other or whether they remain separated by a void, that issue seemed secondary to us. Or rather, as soon as we had accepted the constitution of temporal atoms, we were led to think of them in isolation, realizing that, for the metaphysical clarity of the intuition, we would have to posit a vacuum—whether it existed in fact, or not—in order to imagine a temporal atom properly. It seemed helpful to us, therefore, to compress time around *nodes of action* where being would be recovered in part, while drawing from the mystery of Siloam the creative energy necessary for becoming and progressing.

Finally, in our effort to bring these two doctrines closer to each other, we arrived at a fragmented Bergsonism, at an élan vital that splits up into impulses, at a temporal pluralism that seems to offer—insofar as it accepts a diversity of durations and individual times—a means of analysis as supple as it is rich.

Rarely do metaphysical intuitions erected on an eclectic ideal, however, have an enduring power. A fertile intuition must first of all prove its unity. It was therefore not long before we realized that our conciliatory attempts had managed to marshal the conundrums of both doctrines. A choice had to be made—not at the end of our deliberations, but at the very foundation of these intuitions.

We will now recount how we were able to move from the *atomization of time,* where we had come to take our stand, to the thorough *arithmetization of time,* so steadfastly advanced by Gaston Roupnel.

What had seduced us in the first place, leading us to this recent impasse, was a false conception of the order of metaphysical entities: by retaining our ties with Bergson's thesis, we had intended to introduce duration into the very space of time. Without discussion, we had considered this duration to be the sole quality of time, a synonym of time. We must now admit that such duration is no more than a postulate. And the value of such a postulate can be judged only in terms of the clarity and significance of the theory it favors. Yet we always have the a priori right to start out from a different postulate and try to build a new theory where duration is deduced, rather than postulated.

This a priori consideration would not have been sufficient, however, to lead us back to Roupnel's intuition. For in support of Bergson's concept of duration there were still all the proofs he had assembled regarding the objectivity of duration. Bergson had certainly prompted us to feel duration within ourselves, in an intimate and personal experience. But he went further than that. He objectively demonstrated that we all partake in a single force [élan], that we are all swept along by the same flood tide. Should our boredom or impatience elongate the hour, should joy shorten our day, then impersonal life, other people's lives, would call us back to a fuller and more just appraisal of duration. It would be enough to observe a simple experiment, such as a lump of sugar dissolving in a glass of water, for us to understand that our feeling of duration is corroborated by the existence of an objective and absolute duration. Bergsonian theory thus reclaimed its hold on the field of measurement, even while retaining the evidence of intimate intuition. Although our soul enjoys immediate communication with the *temporal quality* of being, with the essence of becoming, the objectivity of being lies within the domain of *temporal quantity*, however indirect our exploratory access to it may be. Thus everything seemed to safeguard the primacy of duration: intuitive evidence and discursive proofs.

Here, then, is how our own trust in the Bergsonian thesis was undermined.

We were first awakened from our dogmatic slumber by Einstein's critique of objective duration. It quickly became apparent to us that this critique destroyed the absolute of that which endures, while maintaining, as we shall see, the absolute nature of what is—namely, the absolute of the instant.

What Einstein's theory brands with relativity is the *lapse* of time, the "length" of time. The disclosure of such length is actually relative to the chosen method of measurement. We are told that if we take a voyage into outer space and back, at high enough speed, we are bound to discover upon our return that the earth has aged several centuries even while the clock we brought on our voyage has marked but the lapse of a few hours. The voyage required to adjust our impatience to the fixed time Bergson postulates as necessary to melt a piece of sugar in a glass of water would be far shorter, of course.

Let it be clear up front that this is not a matter of idle games of calculation. When it comes to systems in motion, the relativity of elapsed time is henceforth a scientific fact. If we claim the right to reject this aspect of scientific teaching, we should also be allowed to doubt the intervention of physical conditions in the experiment of sugar dissolution, as well as time's effective interference with experimental variables. Doesn't everyone agree, for instance, that temperature plays a role in that experiment with the sugar lump? Very well, then, modern science takes temporal relativity equally into consideration. Science cannot be practiced piecemeal; it must be tackled as a whole.

The rise of relativity theory thus suddenly brought to ruin all arguments that had relied on external proofs of a unique, overarching duration as a fundamental principle for the ordering of events. Metaphysicians were forced to retreat into their own local times and shut themselves up within their own intimate duration. The world did not offer—not immediately at least—any guarantee of convergence for all those individual durations we experience within the intimacy of our consciousness.

What merits special notice, however, is this: *In Einstein's doctrine, the well-specified instant remains an absolute.* To give it this absolute value, suffice it to consider the instant in its synthetic state, as a point in space-time. We ought to take being, in other words, as a synthesis supported at once by space and time. It lies at the convergence point of this place and this moment—*hic et nunc*—not here and tomorrow, nor there and today. In the latter two formulas, the point would dilate along either the temporal axis of duration or the spatial axis of location. Evading a precise synthesis one way or another, each of these formulas would lead to an entirely relative study of duration and space. But once we agree to weld and fuse these two adverbs, the verb "to be" receives at last its full power as an absolute.

It is only in this very place, and at this very moment, that simultaneity can be clear, evident, and precise. Here succession is ordered without hesitation or obscurity. Einstein's doctrine does not allow us to take the simultaneity of two events located at different points in space as self-evident. For such simultaneity to be established definitively, an experiment would be required where one could stand suspended in static ether. Michelson's failure put an end to our hopes of ever realizing such an experiment.[6] Hence we must come up with an *indirect definition* of simultaneity at various locations and, consequently, adjust the measurement of the duration separating different instants to that ever-relative definition of simultaneity. No true concomitance can exist without co-incidence.

We thus return from our incursion into the domain of phenomena with the conviction that duration can only accrue in an artificial way, in a climate of preexisting conventions and definitions, and that its alleged unity comes only from the idle generality of our investigations. The instant reveals itself, on the other hand, as capable of precision and objectivity. We can sense in it the mark of something definite and absolute.

Are we now to turn the *instant* into the compressed center around which we would posit an evanescent duration? Are we to grant the instant, in other words, just enough continuity to give rise to an atom of isolated time, standing out in relief against nothingness—just that vestige of continuity to carve into the Void the two misleading faces of Janus: one looking toward the past, the other toward the future?

Such had been our last attempt before we finally accepted Roupnel's bold and clear-cut argument, entirely without compromise. We now spell out the reason that completed our conversion.

When we still had faith in Bergsonian duration and undertook to study it by distilling and thus impoverishing its contents, our efforts always came up against the same obstacle: we were never able to overcome the prodigal heterogeneity of duration. We of course blamed our failure on nothing but our own inept meditation, our inability to detach ourselves from the continual onslaught of the accidental and the new. We never managed to lose ourselves enough to find ourselves; nor did we succeed in touching and following that uniform flow where duration would unfold a sweeping history without histories, an event without incidents. We would have expected a becoming that was a flight upon a clear sky—a flight displacing nothing, hindered by nothing—the élan in a vacuum. In short, we would have preferred to discover becoming in all its purity and simplicity, becoming in all its solitude. How often we searched for elements in becoming as clear and coherent as those Spinoza had set forth in his meditations on being![7]

But faced with our inability to discover within ourselves those vast lineaments, those smooth sweeping features by which the élan vital is assumed to design becoming, we were naturally led to limit our search for duration's homogeneity within ever-smaller fragments of life. Nonetheless, we kept confronting the same failure: duration was not limited to enduring; it was alive! No matter how small the fragment we considered, a microscopic examination sufficed to reveal a multiplicity of events teeming within it. It was always the embroidering that we encountered, never the plain fabric; always the shadows and reflections upon the river's moving mirror, never the limpid stream. Like substance, duration delivers nothing but phantoms. Duration and substance are, indeed, forever enacting the fable of the deceived deceiver in a hopeless reciprocity with regard to one another: becoming as the phenomenon of substance, substance as the phenomenon of becoming.

Should we not agree, then, that it is metaphysically more prudent to equate time with the accident, which amounts to equating time with its phenomenon? Time is noticed solely through instants; duration—we shall soon see how—is felt solely through instants. Duration is a dust cloud of instants or, better yet, a group of points organized more or less coherently by a *phenomenon* of perspective.[8]

Our need to descend all the way down to temporal points without individual dimension is now evident. For the line that connects the dots and schematizes duration is no more than a panoramic and retrospective function, the indirectly subjective and secondary nature of which we will demonstrate in what follows.

Without intending to develop lengthy psychological proofs, let us here simply note the psychological nature of the problem. The point is to become aware that the *immediate* experience of time is not the experience of duration—elusive, difficult, and abstruse as it is—but rather the sober experience of the instant, apprehended in its immobility. All that is simple and strong in us, even all that is enduring, is the gift of an instant.

To tackle one of the most problematic issues head on, let us start by underscoring the fact that the memory of duration is among the least enduring memories. One remembers having been, but one does not remember having lasted. Since duration depends always on a point of view, temporal distance deforms the perspective of temporal length. Besides, what is pure memory in Bergsonian philosophy if not an image taken in its isolation? Had we leisure enough to study, in a longer work, the problem of how memories are located in time, we would have no trouble showing how poorly positioned they are, how artificially they find an order within our intimate history. Halbwachs's fine book on "the social frameworks of memory" sets out to prove that our meditation lacks any solid psychological structure, a stable skeleton of dead duration that would allow us—naturally, psychologically, and in the solitude of our own consciousness[9]—to pinpoint the place of an evoked memory. Ultimately, we need to learn and relearn our own chronology. And to aid us in this task, we resort to all kinds of historical accounts or synoptic tables, veritable summaries of the most fortuitous coincidences. This is how the story of kings comes to be inscribed in the humblest of hearts. Were we less attentive to contemporary history, we would have a muddled view of our own history or, at the very least, it would be full of anachronisms. It is through an election as insignificant as that of a nation's president that we can quickly and precisely locate the intimate memory of a time when we risked the destiny of our heart. But if the process of locating memories is so obviously indirect a task—if, to be accurate, we must extend our references to domains far removed from our intimate life[10]—isn't this proof enough that we have not retained the least trace of deceased durations? Memory, that guardian of time, guards the instant alone. It preserves nothing, absolutely nothing, of our complicated and artificial sense of duration.

The psychology of will and attention—that will of intelligence—likewise prepares us to accept the Roupnelian notion of the durationless instant as a working hypothesis. This psychology had already made it clear to us that duration can only intervene indirectly; it is fairly easy to see that it is not a primordial condition: with duration we might perhaps be able to measure waiting [*l'attente*], but not attention itself [*l'attention*],[11] which receives its entire intensity value within a single instant.

This problem of attention naturally became an issue at the very level of our meditations on duration. Since we were personally unable to focus long enough upon that ideal nothing representing the bare self, we were unavoidably tempted to break duration down into the rhythm of our acts of attention. And there again, faced with the minimum of unexpectedness as we attempted to rediscover the realm of pure and plain inwardness, we suddenly realized that this attention to ourselves delivered, all by itself, the delightful and fragile novelties of a thought without history, a thought without thoughts. Focused entirely on the Cartesian cogito, such thought has no duration. Its evidence rests on its instantaneous character alone; it is clearly conscious of itself only insofar as it is empty and solitary. So it awaits [*elle attend*] the world's attack within a duration that is but a void of thought, therefore a de facto void. The world brings it an experience. And it is once again in a fertile instant that attentive consciousness will become enriched with objective knowledge.

Yet since attention has both the need and the power to recapture itself, it is in essence to be found entirely in its resumptions. Attention is also a series of beginnings; it is constituted by those mental rebirths that occur in consciousness when it heeds time's instants. And if we carried our examination deeper into that narrow region where attention becomes decision, we would begin to appreciate the lightning quality of a will in which clarity of motive and the joy of acting suddenly converge. Only then could we truly speak of instantaneous conditions. Such conditions are strictly preliminary, or better yet preinitial, for they precede what geometricians call the initial conditions of movement. This is indeed what renders them metaphysically, not abstractly, instantaneous. If you watch a cat stalking its prey, you will be able to see the *instant of attack* suddenly inscribe itself upon reality, while Bergsonians tend to follow the trajectory of attack no matter how tightly focused their scrutiny of duration may be. Once triggered, the cat's pounce will of course develop a duration sequence according to the laws of physics and physiology—laws that regulate complex functions. But before the complicated process of the leap is actually set off, there has already been a simple, brutal instant of decision.

Furthermore, if we direct this attention to the spectacle that surrounds us—if we consider it as attention to life rather than to private thought—we will immediately realize that attention is always born of coincidence. Such a chance event is the minimum of novelty necessary to focus the mind. If duration were the sole principle of order and differentiation of events, we would never be able to pay attention to a process of development. Novelty is needed for thought to intervene; novelty is also needed for consciousness to affirm itself and for life to progress. And of course novelty is, in principle, always instantaneous.

Finally, it is the point of space-time that would best help us analyze the psychology of will, perceptual evidence, and attention. Unfortunately, for such analysis to become clear and convincing, philosophical language and even ordinary language would need to have assimilated the doctrines of relativity theory. Although this assimilation is already underway, we sense that it is still far from reaching completion. Nonetheless, we believe it is along this path that the fusion of spatial atomism and temporal atomism will be accomplished. The more intimate this fusion, the better we shall appreciate the value of Roupnel's thesis. It is in this way that its concrete character will best be grasped. The space-time-consciousness complex constitutes the triple essence of atomism; it is the monad affirmed in its triple solitude—without communication with other things, other times, or other souls.

But these claims will appear all the more dubious as they go against the grain of our habits of thought and expression. We are well aware that they will not be immediately convincing. Indeed, to many readers, the field of psychology may seem hardly favorable ground for pursuing such metaphysical investigations.

What did we hope to achieve by assembling all these arguments? Simply to show that we would welcome debate, even in the most unfavorable of terrains. Yet since it is the problem's metaphysical argument that is ultimately the strongest, we shall now focus our energies in that direction. In its barest outline, Roupnel's temporal intuition affirms two basic tenets:

(1) the absolutely discontinuous character of time; and

(2) the absolutely punctiform character of the instant.

Roupnel's thesis indeed brings about the most complete and candid arithmetization of time. Duration is but a number whose unit is the instant.

For greater clarity let us restate, as a corollary, our denial of the truly temporal and immediate character of duration. Roupnel writes: "Space and Time only appear infinite to us when they do not exist" (*Siloë*, 126). Francis Bacon had already remarked that nothing is vaster than empty things.[12] Inspired by such formulas, we believe we can say without deforming Roupnel's thought that *only nothingness is truly continuous.*

IV

In formulating this phrase, we are well aware of the objections it is bound to provoke. We will be told that the nothingness of time is precisely the interval that separates those instants marked out by events. To defeat us even more decisively, our opponents will grant us that events have an instantaneous birth and—if they must—that they are instantaneous. But an interval, they will argue, must have a real existence to be distinguished from instants. We will be pressed to concede that this interval is indeed time—empty time, time without events, time that endures, duration that prolongs itself, duration that can be measured. Still, we will persist in affirming that time is nothing if nothing constitutes it, that eternity[13] before creation makes no sense, that nothingness cannot be measured and in fact has no dimensions whatsoever.

Our wholly arithmetized intuition of time—opposed as it is to popular theory, hence so likely to clash with commonly held ideas—ought nevertheless to be judged on its own merits. While this intuition may seem lowly, one should at least recognize that up to this point it has remained coherent with itself in all its developments.

If moreover we can introduce a principle that establishes a substitute for the measurement of time, we believe we will have crossed a critical threshold, probably the last that still awaits us.

Let us spell out that criticism as bluntly as possible.

Your thesis, we will be told, cannot admit time's measurement any more than it can allow for time's proportional subdivisions. And yet you—along with everyone else—say that an hour lasts sixty minutes, and that a minute takes sixty seconds. You must therefore believe in duration. You cannot speak without using all those adverbs, all those words that evoke what endures, what passes by, what is awaited. You are forced, in your own discussion, to say: for a long time, meanwhile, during. Duration is ingrained in our grammar—in morphology as much as in our syntax.

Words are indeed there before thought, before our efforts to renew thought. We have to make use of them as they are. But is it not the role of the philosopher to deform the meaning of words enough to draw the abstract from the concrete, to allow thought to escape from things? Is it not the philosopher's task—as is the poet's—"to give a purer sense to the language of the tribe" (Mallarmé)?[14] And if critics are willing to reflect on the fact that all words that translate temporal qualities are involved in metaphors—insofar as their radicals are partly drawn from spatial elements—they will realize that we have not been disarmed on the polemic field, and the charge that we are engaging in a verbal vicious circle will have to be dropped.

But the problem of measurement remains unchallenged, and that is evidently where the critique against our position must appear decisive. If duration is *measured*, it is because it has a certain magnitude. Duration thus bears the overt sign of its reality.

So let us now ascertain whether or not this sign is truly immediate, and attempt to show how, in our view, Roupnel's intuition might construe duration.

What, then, gives time the appearance of continuity? It would, in fact, seem that by inserting a temporal break *any time we want* along the continuum, we are able to pinpoint a phenomenon that illustrates the arbitrarily designated instant. We would thus feel assured that our act of knowledge is open to full and free inspection. In other words, we claim to place our acts of freedom upon a continuous line *because we can experience the efficacy of our acts at any moment.* We seem certain of all this, but of this alone.

To state the same idea in slightly different language—which, at first glance, may seem synonymous with the first—we will instead say *every time we want to, we can experience the efficacy of our acts.*

Here comes an objection. Doesn't the first way of expressing ourselves tacitly presuppose the continuity of our being? And isn't this continuity assumed to issue from the self we bring to our account of duration? But what guarantee do we have of the continuity thus attributed to ourselves? For our inspection to succeed at every stroke, the rhythm of our disjointed being need only correspond to *one* beat of the cosmos. More explicitly, all that is needed to prove the arbitrary nature of our break is for the *occasion* of our intimate action to correspond to one event of the universe—in short, for a coincidence to occur at one point in space-time-consciousness. Consequently—and this is our key argument—the expression *every time* in the thesis of discontinuous time appears to be the exact synonym of the expression *any time* in the thesis of continuous time. If one is willing to allow this translation, then the whole language of continuity is placed at our disposal through this new key.

Life places such a prodigious wealth of instants at our disposal, moreover, that it seems by all accounts inexhaustible. And, realizing that we could spend much more of this wealth, we tend to believe we could lavishly spend our moments without counting—hence our impression of intimate, unbroken continuity.

Once we have understood the importance of a concomitance expressed by an agreement of instants, the interpretation of synchronism becomes clear in Roupnel's hypothesis of discontinuity. Here again, a comparison needs to be established between Bergson's intuitions and those of Roupnel:

"Two phenomena are synchronous," Bergsonian philosophers will say, "if they are *always* in temporal unison." It is a matter of calibrating becomings and actions.

"Two phenomena are synchronous," Roupnelian philosophers will say, "if *every time* the first is present, the second is equally present." It is a matter of calibrating fresh starts and acts.

Which is the more prudent formula?

To say, with Bergson, that synchronism corresponds to the parallel unfolding of two event sequences is slightly to overstep the domains of objective proof and verification. We reject such a metaphysical extrapolation that asserts a *continuum in itself,* when we are in fact constantly facing the discontinuity of our own experience. Synchronism, therefore, always appears in a concordant numeration of effective instants, and never as a geometric measure of continuous duration.

At this juncture we will be held up no doubt by yet another objection: we will be told that, once we have admitted that an entire phenomenon might be studied by following the precise temporal schema of a cinematic shot, we cannot deny that a division of time remains possible, even desirable, if we hope to follow the phenomenon's development in all its meanderings. Our critics will obviously allude here to some ultramodern motion picture camera that registers the process of becoming in the ten-thousandths of a second. Why then should we be restricted in the division of time?

The reason why our opponents posit an endless division of time is that they initially frame their analysis at the level of an entire life summed up by the curve of the élan vital. Since from a macroscopic perspective we live what appears to be an unbroken or continuous duration, a close examination of details would induce us, in their view, to appreciate duration in ever-smaller fractions than our initially chosen units.

But the problem would change meaning if we considered the actual construction of time starting from instants, instead of its artificial division starting from duration. We would then see that time multiplies itself following the schema of numerical correspondences, far from dividing itself according to the fragmentation schema of some continuum.

Besides, the word "fraction" is itself ambiguous. Here it would help, in our view, to recall Couturat's summary of fraction theory.[15] A fraction is the grouping of two whole numbers in which the denominator does not really divide the numerator. The difference between advocates of temporal continuity and ourselves regarding this arithmetical aspect of the problem can be summed up as follows:

For the purposes of analysis, our opponents start from the numerator, which they take to be a homogeneous, continuous quantity, and above all an immediately given quantity. They divide this "given" by the denominator, which is thus delivered to the arbitrary nature of the test—all the more arbitrary the more fine-tuned the test. Should they push their infinitesimal analysis too far, our opponents might even risk "dissolving" duration altogether.

We start from the denominator, on the other hand, as mark of the phenomenon's wealth of instants and our basis for comparison. Of course, this rich phenomenon is intuited with the utmost subtlety[16]—our wager being that it would be absurd for the measuring instrument to be less subtle than the phenomenon to be measured.[17] On this basis, we wonder then how often the actualization of a slower, looser phenomenon happens to coincide with instants within this finely scanned phenomenon. The successes of synchronism are what finally yield the numerator of the fraction.

The two fractions thus constructed may yield the same value. But they are not constructed the same way.

We are certainly aware of the tacit objection bound to arise at this point: to determine the number of successes, wouldn't it be necessary for a mysterious orchestra conductor to beat time beyond and above the two rhythms being compared? In other words, critics will say, aren't you concerned that the word *during,* which you have avoided voicing so far, is tacitly used in your own analysis? Indeed, the major difficulty of Roupnel's thesis lies in avoiding terms drawn from the mainstream psychology of duration. But again, if we are willing to meditate by going from the phenomenon rich in instants to the phenomenon poor in instants—i.e., from denominator to numerator, and not the reverse—we will realize that we can get along not only without words that evoke the idea of duration (a mere verbal feat), but even without the idea of duration itself, all of which proves that duration could at best play the role of servant in the domain where she used to rule as mistress.

For greater clarity, however, let us create a diagram of this correspondence. Following this diagram, we will develop two readings—one in the language of duration, and the other in the language of instants—*remaining at all times within the Roupnelian perspective, even as we perform this double reading.*

Let us suppose the macroscopic phenomenon can be depicted by this first line of dots:

1.   .   .   .   .   .

We place these dots without regard for the interval separating them, since it is not from the interval, in our view, that duration derives its sense or its schema. For us the continuous interval is nothingness; and nothingness has no more "length" than it has duration.

With equal reservations, we now depict the more finely scanned phenomenon by a second line of dots:

2.   . . .   .

Let us now compare the two diagrams.

If we now undertake to read as advocates of continuity—from top to bottom (a Roupnelian reading, nonetheless)—we will say that *while* "phenomenon 1" occurs one time, "phenomenon 2" occurs three times. We will appeal to a duration that dominates the series—a duration which grants meaning to our word "while" and becomes increasingly ostensible in ever cruder domains, such as those of the minute, the hour, the day . . .

If, on the contrary, we read synchronism as uncompromising advocates of discontinuity—from bottom to top—we will say that the phenomena of multiple chance-events (which are closest to real time) correspond to one phenomenon of macroscopic time, one out of three times.

Though the two readings may be ultimately equivalent, the first is a bit too dependent on surface appearance, too impressionistic, whereas the second corresponds more closely to the primordial text.

Let us elaborate this thought through a musical metaphor. While in the world's orchestra there are instruments that often fall silent, it is false to say there is *always* some instrument playing. The world is conducted in keeping with a musical measure imposed by the cadence of instants. If we could hear all the instants of reality, we would understand that an eighth note is not made up from fragments of a half note but, rather, that a half note *repeats* the eighth note. It is from such repetition that the *impression* of continuity is born.

Henceforth we realize that the relative richness of instants sets up for us a sort of relative measure of time. To be able to give an accurate account of our temporal fortune, that is, to measure everything that repeats itself in us, we would truly have to experience all of time's instants. Only within such a totality could a veritable display of discontinuous time be obtained, and only in the monotony of repetition could the impression of empty, hence pure, duration be discovered. Founded upon a numerical comparison with the totality of instants, the concept of the temporal richness of a particular life or phenomenon would then take on an absolute sense, according to the way in which this richness is utilized or, rather, fails to be fully realized. Such an absolute foundation being denied us, however, we must be content with relative assessments.

The way is thus being paved toward a concept of "rich duration" which should serve the same ends as "extended duration." Such a concept could account not only for facts but above all for illusions—a crucial factor from a psychological perspective, since the life of mind is illusion before it is thought.[18] We recognize as well that our constant, ceaselessly regained illusions are no longer pure illusions, and that as we meditate on our errors we come closer to the truth. La Fontaine was right in speaking of illusions "that never deceive by always lying to us."[19]

The harsh rigors of learned metaphysics can thus be slackened, allowing us to return to the shores of Siloam where mind and heart become reconciled as they complement each other. The affective character of duration—the joy or pain of being—derives from the proportion or disproportion of living hours used as time for thought, or time for feeling. Matter neglects being, life neglects living, and the heart neglects loving. It is in slumber that we lose paradise. But let us delve more deeply into the scenario of our idleness: an atom radiates with frequency, and hence exists by using a great number, though never all, of its instants. A living cell is already more sparing in its efforts, using a mere fraction of the temporal possibilities furnished by the ensemble of atoms that constitute it. As for thought, it is by irregular flashes that it utilizes life. Three types of filters through which all too few instants can emerge into consciousness! And so the shadow of mute suffering stalks us whenever we go *in search of lost instants.*[20] Yes, we recall those rich hours marked by the endless pealing of Easter bells, those bells of resurrection whose strokes we never count because they all count, because they each give rise to an echo in our awakened soul. But this joyful remembrance readily turns into remorse as soon as we compare those hours of full life to the slow intellectual hours, relatively sparse as they are; to the dead empty hours, so empty of purpose as Carlyle would lament; to the unending hostile hours, as they yield nothing.

And so we dream of a divine hour that would bestow everything. Not the *replete hour,* but the *complete hour.* The hour where all instants of time would be utilized by matter, the hour where all instants realized by matter would be utilized by life, the hour where all living instants would be felt, loved, thought—hence, the hour where the relativity of consciousness would fade away, for consciousness would now be commensurate with the fullness of time.

Ultimately, *objective time is maximal time*—that time which, containing each and every instant, is composed of the richly dense ensemble of the Creator's acts.

V

We have yet to offer an account of the vectorial character of duration, to indicate what it is that gives time its sense of direction. How can a perspective of vanished instants be called *past,* and how can a perspective of expectation be called *future?*

If we have been able to shed some light on the core intuition proposed by Roupnel, then we must be ready to admit that past and future— like duration—correspond to impressions that are essentially secondary and indirect. Past and future do not affect the essence of being, even less the primary essence of time. For Roupnel, we repeat, time is the instant, and it is the present instant that bears the full weight of temporality. The past is as empty as the future. The future is as dead as the past. The instant holds no duration at its core; it does not thrust a force in one direction or another. It does not have two faces. It is whole and alone. We may meditate on its essence as much as we wish, but we will not find in the instant the root of a necessary and sufficient duality for us to think a directional vector.

As soon as we agree to follow Roupnel's inspiration in meditating on the instant, moreover, we realize that the present does not *pass,* for we forsake an instant only to find another. Consciousness is consciousness of the instant, and consciousness of the instant is consciousness: two formulas so akin to each other that they place us within the closest of reciprocities, ensuring the integration of pure consciousness and temporal reality. Once seized in solitary meditation, consciousness becomes as motionless as the isolated instant.

It is in the isolation of the instant that time can assume its poor yet pure homogeneity. And this homogeneity of the instant does not in any way disprove the anisotropy[21] that results from diverse groupings of instants—concatenations that allow the mind to recover the individuality of durations, so well highlighted by Bergson. In other words, since there is nothing within an instant itself that allows us to postulate duration, and nothing that could immediately account for our experience—quite real nonetheless—of what we call past and future, we must therefore attempt to construct the perspective of instants that alone can designate the past and the future.

When listening carefully to the symphony of instants, we happen to sense certain phrases dying off, phrases falling and being swept away toward the past. But such a flight toward the past—by the very fact that it is a secondary appearance—is entirely relative. One rhythm fades away in relation to another section of the symphony that continues. Such a gradual and relative decline may be roughly represented by the following diagram:

. . .   . .   .

. . . .

The three-to-five ratio *becomes* two-to-five, one-to-five, and then silence—the silence of a being that departs, even as the surrounding world continues to resonate.

This diagram may help us understand what is simultaneously both potential and relative in what we generally call the present time (without specifying boundaries). A rhythm that persists unchanged is a present that has duration. This lasting present is constituted by multiple instants which, from one particular standpoint, are assured of perfect monotony. The enduring feelings that shape the individuality of a particular soul are spun out of these very monotonies. Unification may arise even in the midst of highly diverse circumstances. For the person who continues to love, a lost love is both present and past—present for the faithful heart, past for the unhappy heart. Thus, for a heart capable of accepting suffering and fond recollection at the same time, a lost love is both pain and solace. This amounts to saying that a permanent love—sign of an enduring soul—is something other than suffering and happiness, and that in transcending this affective contradiction, a feeling that endures takes on a metaphysical quality. A loving soul truly experiences the solidarity of instants that are repeated with regularity. Conversely, a uniform rhythm of instants is an *a priori form* of affection.

The inverse of the first diagram would depict a nascent rhythm, while furnishing elements of the relative measure of its progress. The musical ear hears the destiny of a melody, knowing how a phrase that has begun will fulfill itself. We fore-hear the future of a sound, just as we foresee the future of a trajectory. We strain ourselves and direct all our forces toward the immediate future. It is this tension that constitutes our actual sense of duration. As Guyau once said, it is our intention that truly organizes the future as a perspective in which we are the center of projection: "We must desire, wish, will, extend a hand, and march ahead to create the future. The future is not *that which comes toward us*, but *that toward which we move*" (*Genèse*, 33). Both the sense and scope of the future are thus inscribed within the present itself.[22]

We indeed build in time, as we build in space. There is a metaphorical persistence in this view, however, that calls for further elucidation. We will then come to recognize that the memory of the past and the anticipation of the future are actually founded upon habits. Since the past is but a memory and the future but a prediction, we will argue that both past and future are essentially no more than habits. And these, we might add, are far from being the immediate habits ingrained at an early age. Ultimately, in our view, the qualities that make time seem to endure— much as those that delineate time in terms of past and future perspectives—are not properties of time's primary aspect. A philosopher must reconstruct them on the basis of the sole temporal reality given immediately to thought—namely, the reality of the *instant*.

All the difficulties of *Siloë* are centered on this point, as we shall see. But these difficulties may stem from readers' preconceived ideas. If readers are first willing to get a firm grasp of both ends of the dilemma we are trying to resolve, they will come to understand our line of reasoning. The two apparently conflicting conclusions that we must hence reconcile can be summed up as follows:

> 1. Duration has no direct force. Real time exists only through the isolated instant, which is to be found wholly in the act, in what is actual, in the present.

> 2. Being is nonetheless a site of resonance by virtue of the rhythms of instants. As such, one might say that being has a past, much as an echo has a voice. Yet this past is no more than a present habit, and this present state of the past is, again, but a metaphor. For us, in fact, habit is inscribed neither in matter nor in space. What is at issue is simply a resonant habit that, we believe, remains essentially relative. Habit, which in our view is thought, turns out to be too ethereal to become permanently recorded, too immaterial to sleep within matter. It is a movement that keeps playing, a musical phrase that must be taken up again, for it forms part of a symphony where it plays a role. At least, this is the way we will attempt to reconcile past and future, through habit.

Rhythm is naturally less reliable on the side of the future. Between yesterday's nothingness and tomorrow's nothingness there is no symmetry. The future is but a prelude, a musical phrase that proceeds and tries itself out—a solitary phrase. It is only through such a brief overture that the world prolongs itself. In the symphony that is being created, the future is assured by but a few musical measures.

For human beings, the asymmetry between past and future is radical. In us, the past is a voice that has found an echo. We thus attribute a force to what is no more than a form—or better yet, we assign one sweeping form to a plurality of forms. It is through such a synthesis that the past begins to take on the weight of reality.

But the future, no matter how far-reaching our desire, is a perspective without depth. It has no reliable link to reality. That is why we say that the future is in God's hands.

These ideas are likely to become clearer once we are able to summarize the second theme of Roupnel's philosophy—namely, the theme of habit, to which he granted first place in his essay. If we have shifted the order of our analysis, it is because the absolute negation of the reality of the past is the daunting postulate to be acknowledged before the challenge of assimilating it into current ideas on habit can be reasonably assessed. In short, the point of our next chapter will be to explore how the standard psychology of habit can be reconciled with a thesis that denies the direct and immediate effect of the past upon the present instant.

VI

Before tackling the problem of habit, we could however search the field of contemporary science for further evidence to support the intuition of discontinuous time, if that were our main goal. Roupnel himself did not fail to draw a connection between his thesis of temporal discontinuity and the modern description of radiation phenomena in quantum theory (see *Siloë*, 121). The computation of atomic energy is ultimately established by employing arithmetic rather than geometry. As the language of *"how often"* gradually replaces the language of *"how long,"* this computation is expressed in frequencies, rather than in durations.

Nonetheless, at the time he was writing, Roupnel could hardly foresee the far-reaching implications of the theories on temporal discontinuity presented at the Congress of the Solvay Institute in 1927. Even as we now read the most recent works on atomic statistics, we cannot help but notice that the fundamental element of these statistics remains elusive. What is it that needs to be tallied: electrons, quanta, packets of energy?

Where should the root of individuality be located? It is not absurd to reach as far back as temporal reality itself in order to find the primary element mobilized by chance. Then a statistical conception of fertile instants—each one taken independently and in isolation from one another—would in fact be conceivable.

Some interesting connections could also be established between the problem of the atom's positive existence and its essentially instantaneous manifestation. In certain respects, radiation phenomena could well be interpreted by saying that an atom exists only at the moment it changes. And if we added that such change occurs abruptly, we would be led to admit that everything that is real is condensed in the instant. The atom's energy needs to be accounted for in terms of sudden pulses rather than velocities.

Conversely, by showing the importance of the instant in the event, we could reveal the weakness of the frequent objection regarding the so-called reality of the "interval" separating two instants. For statistical conceptions of time, the interval between two instants is nothing but an interval of probability. The more protracted the void, the greater the chance an instant will bring it to an end. It is this intensification of chance that truly measures its magnitude. Empty duration, pure duration has therefore but one magnitude: potentiality. From the moment it ceases to radiate, the atom passes into a completely virtual energetic existence. It no longer consumes anything; the speed of its electrons uses up no material energy. In this virtual state, it no longer even conserves power that might be released after a period of long repose. It is truly nothing more than an abandoned toy; even less, the atom is but a formal rule in a game that organizes mere possibilities. Of course, chance will eventually restore existence to the atom. In other words, the atom will receive the gift of a fertile instant, but it will receive it by chance, as an essential novelty according to the laws of probability calculus. For it is necessary that sooner or later the universe in all its aspects have a share in temporal reality. The possible is indeed a temptation to which the real will always give way in the end.

Chance incites, however, without binding with absolute necessity. It is thus understandable that time should provide the illusion of inevitable action even when, in truth, it has no real action. If an atom happens to remain inactive on a number of occasions, even as its neighboring atoms keep radiating, the turn for this long-quiescent, isolated atom to act will become increasingly probable. Repose enhances the probability of action, even though it does not really prepare for action. Duration does not behave "like a cause,"[23] but rather *like a chance*. Here, again, *the principle of causality is better expressed in terms of the numeration of acts than in terms of the geometry of protracted actions.*

But all such scientific proofs lie beyond the scope of our present inquiry. Were we to elaborate on them, we would distract readers from our goal. For the main task we wish to undertake here is that of liberation through intuition. Since the intuition of continuity can at times be oppressive, it is certainly useful to attempt interpreting phenomena through the inverse intuition. Whatever one might think of the strength of our evidence, the value of exploring an array of different intuitions at the foundation of philosophy and science cannot be denied. In reading Roupnel's book, we ourselves were struck by the lesson of intuitive independence that might be achieved by exploring and developing a challenging intuition. It is through the dialectic of intuitions that one can best benefit from intuitions without the risk of being blinded by them. Philosophically understood, the intuition of discontinuous time will aid readers who wish to pursue the implications of discontinuity theories in the most diverse areas of the physical sciences. Time is what is most difficult to conceive in terms of discontinuous form. Therefore, a meditation on the temporal discontinuity realized by the *isolated instant* is what promises to open the most direct pathways to a pedagogy of discontinuity.

2

The Problem of Habit and Discontinuous Time

Every soul is a melody to be renewed.
—Mallarmé, "Entretien avec Stéphane Mallarmé"

I

The above-mentioned problem of habit seems insoluble, at first glance, from the standpoint of the temporal thesis we have just developed. We have actually denied the real persistence of the past. We have shown that the past would be entirely dead the moment the new instant affirmed the real. And so, in keeping with the idea usually held about habit, we will be compelled to reinvest habit—that legacy of a departed past—with the force that gives being a stable appearance under a mutable becoming. One might therefore suspect we have wandered into a dead-end alley. Yet by trusting Roupnel's lead on this difficult terrain, we will find our way back to the main arteries of fertile philosophical intuitions.

Roupnel himself indicates the character of his task: "We must now invest the atom with realities we have removed from Space and Time, and draw lessons from the shattered remains of these two despoilers of the Temple" (*Siloë*, 127). Roupnel's attack against the ostensible reality of continuous space is no less vigorous, in fact, than the attack we have just retraced against the so-called reality of duration understood as an immediate continuity. For Roupnel, the atom has *spatial properties* in the same way, and as indirectly, as it has chemical properties. In other words, an atom does not become substantive by appropriating a piece of space

---

Mallarmé's line "*Toute âme est une mélodie qu'il s'agit de renouer*" is found in "Entretien avec Stéphane Mallarmé," text drawn from *Carnets de voyages de Sofia—L'âme des poètes*, by Angela Columberg. See http://poesies.poemes.free.fr/entretien-sofia-mallarme.php.

that would serve as a framework for the real. All it does is display itself spatially. The structure of the atom simply organizes separate points, just as its becoming organizes isolated instants. The solidarity of forces of being are not truly borne by space, any more than they are borne by time. *Elsewhere* does not act upon *here*, any more than *formerly* acts upon *now*.

When considered from the outside, being is doubly blocked within the solitude of the instant and the point. As we have seen, as soon as we attempt to grasp being from within, the solitude of consciousness is added to this redoubled physical solitude. How could we fail to find here a corroboration of Leibnizian intuitions! Leibniz denied the direct and active solidarity of beings distributed in space. Instead, his notion of a preestablished harmony assumed at the heart of each monad a veritable continuity realized by the action of a universal and absolute time through which the perfect concordance of all monads would be illustrated. We find in *Siloë* an additional negation: the denial of the *direct* solidarity of present being with past being. But, once again, if such solidarity of temporal instants is neither direct nor given—if, in other words, it is not duration which immediately links instants gathered in groups according to certain principles, it becomes more urgent than ever to show how a nondirect, nontemporal solidarity manifests itself in the becoming of being. In short, we must find a principle to replace the hypothesis of preestablished harmony. It is toward this principle that, we believe, the Roupnelian theses of habit are oriented.

Our challenge will be, first of all, to demonstrate that habit is still conceivable, even when removed from its dependence on a past that is postulated, without good or sufficient reason, as directly efficacious.[1] We must then show that habit, defined this time in terms of the intuition of isolated instants, explains at once the permanence of being and its progress. But let us first take a brief parenthetical detour.

If our position is problematic, that of our opponents is by contrast surprisingly effortless. Notice, for instance, how everything appears to be simple from the standpoint of realistic thinking, the thinking that "realizes" all things. To begin with, being is conceived fundamentally as substance—substance that is at once, by definition, the support of qualities and the support of becoming. Leaving a trace within matter, the past is reflected in the present and hence remains materially alive. The future of a germ-seed appears to be materially prepared and anticipated as efficiently as a brain cell that retains a memory. Insofar as habit is concerned, it is useless to explain it, for it is habit that explains everything. Suffice it to say that the brain is a storehouse of motor schemas to convince us that habit is a mechanism placed at being's disposal by former efforts. Habit will hence differentiate the matter of being to the point of organizing the solidarity of past and future. What is the *key word* that sheds light on this realistic psychology? It is the word that translates *an inscription*. From the moment one states that the past, or habit, is *inscribed* within matter, everything is explained. There is no longer any question.

We must demand more of ourselves. An inscription does not explain anything, in our view. So let us begin by formulating our objections against the material action of the present instant upon future instants, such as the seed supposedly exercises in the transmission of its vital forms. No doubt, as Roupnel observes,

> [it is] a particularly facile linguistic expedient to invest the *germ cell* with all the promises the individual is bound to realize, and to charge it with the collective patrimony of habits that will carry out the being's forms and functions. But when we say the *totality* of these habits is contained within the *germ cell*, we must be careful to understand the implications of that phrase, or rather the very value of that image. Nothing could be more dangerous than to imagine the *germ cell* as a container whose contents are a group of properties. Such association of the abstract and the concrete is impossible, besides the fact that it explains nothing. (*Siloë*, 34)

It is instructive to compare Roupnel's critique, here, with a metaphysical objection presented by Alexandre Koyré in his analysis of mystical thought:

> We would like to insist, however, on the idea of the *germ* that one finds implied or expressed in every organicist doctrine. The very idea of the germ is a *mysterium*. It concentrates in itself, so to speak, all the particularities of organicist thought. It is a veritable union of opposites, even contradictions. The germ, one might say, is what it is not. It already is what it is not yet, and only what it will be. It is that, for otherwise it could not become so. It is not that, for otherwise how could it become so? The germ is at once both the *matter* that evolves and the *power* that makes it evolve. The germ acts upon itself. It is a *causa sui:* if not of its own being, at least of its development. It indeed seems that understanding is incapable of seizing this concept: in linear logic, the organic circle of life necessarily transforms itself into a vicious circle.[2]

The reason for this mélange of contradictions comes no doubt from the fact that it combines two different definitions of substance which must simultaneously hold true for both being and becoming, the real instant and perceived duration, the concrete and the constructed, or better yet, as Roupnel puts it, the concrete and the abstract.

If the effect of the present instant upon future instants in the generation of living beings remains unclear—even while a normative scheme may be conceivable—how much more prudent should we be when postulating the inscription of thousands of confused and blurred events from the past within matter that is charged with actualizing by-gone time.

In the first place, why should a nerve cell register certain events and not others? To be more precise, if there is no normative or aesthetic action, how could habit conserve a rule and a form?[3] We are always faced with the same debate. Partisans of duration feel no compunction about multiplying and prolonging temporal actions. They want to benefit simultaneously from the gradual continuity of the action, and from the discontinuity of an action that would remain latent, waiting throughout its duration for the proper instant to be reborn. In their view, it is as much by enduring as it is by repeating itself that a habit gets reinforced. Partisans of discontinuous time are, on the other hand, struck by the novelty of fertile instants that grant habit its suppleness and efficacy. It is above all by the attack of habit that they would explain its function and persistence, much as the attack of a violin bow is what determines the subsequent sound. Habit can utilize energy only if this energy is plucked, following a particular rhythm. It is in this sense that one might inter-pret the Roupnelian formula: "Energy is but a great memory" (Siloë, 10). Energy can in fact be brought into play only through memory. It is the memory of a rhythm.

Thus, in our view, habit is always an act restituted in its novelty. The consequences and development of this act are handed over to sub-ordinate habits—less rich, no doubt—which expend their own energy by obeying the primordial acts that govern them. Samuel Butler had already remarked that memory is principally affected by two forces of opposite character, namely, "the force of novelty, and the force of rou-tine—through incidents or objects which are either the most familiar or the least familiar to us."[4] Faced with these two forces—novelty and rou-tine—being reacts synthetically rather than dialectically, hence our pro-posed definition of habit as a routine assimilation of novelty. But this no-tion of routine should not suggest an inferior sort of automatism, which would expose us to the charge of falling into a vicious circle. Rather, the relativity of perspectives intervenes in this case, for as soon as we apply our examination to the domain of routine, we come to realize that rou-tine itself—no less than the most active intellectual habits—is nourished by the vital force of the radical novelty of *instants*.

Examine the play of hierarchically ordered habits, and you will notice that a special skill cannot endure as a skill unless it strives to surpass itself, unless it progresses. If the pianist does not wish to perform better today than he did yesterday, he will abandon himself to less polished habits. If he fails to return periodically to the musical piece, his fingers will soon lose the habit of gliding across the keyboard. It is truly the soul that leads the hand. To seize habit in its essence, it is therefore necessary to seize it in its growth. Thus, by its incremental successes, habit becomes the synthesis of novelty and routine, and that synthesis is crystallized through fertile instants.[5]

From here, we can see how great creations—such as the creation of a living being—would require the presence of matter that is fresh in some way,[6] matter ready from the outset to welcome the advent of novelty with faith. Hence the word that issues from Butler's pen:

> No conjecture can be hazarded as to how the smallest particle of matter became so imbued with faith that it must be considered as the beginning of *Life*, or as to what such faith is, except that it is the very essence of all things, and that it has no foundation.[7]

This faith is *everything*, one might say, for it operates at the very level of the synthesis of instants; but it is substantially *nothing* since it claims to transcend the reality of the instant. Here again faith is expectation and novelty. There is nothing less conventional than faith in life. A being that offers itself to life, in its passion for novelty, is itself inclined to welcome the present as a promise of the future. The greatest of all forces is the power of naïveté. Roupnel granted special emphasis to that state of meditative concentration wherein lies the germ that gives rise to life. He understood the extent of affirmative freedom in an absolute beginning. The germ is no doubt a being that imitates and reproduces, in certain respects, but it can do so only in the exuberance of a new beginning. Its true function is to begin. "The *germ cell* bears within itself nothing but the beginning of cellular procreation" (*Siloë*, 33). In other words, *a germ cell is the beginning of a habit of life*. If we read "continuity" into the propagation of a species, it is because our reading is rudimentary. We take individuals as manifestations of evolution, when they are in fact its *agents*. Roupnel rightly brushes aside all the more or less materialistic principles proposed to assure the formal continuity of living beings.

> We seem to have been able to reason as if *germ cells* did not constitute discontinuous elements. We have invested the gamete with the heritage of ages as if it had been present throughout its entire course. But let

us declare, once and for all, that the theory of representative particles
has nothing to do with the theory we are now proposing. It is not at all
necessary to introduce elements into a gamete that would have served
as constant bearers of the past and eternal agents of becoming. In order
to play the role we attribute to it, the gamete has no need of Naegeli's
micelles, Darwin's *gemmules,* de Vriès's *pangenes,* or Weissmann's *germina-
tive plasma.* It needs only itself, its immediate substance and virtue, its
moment. It lives and dies entirely in contemporaneity. It gathers the
heritage peculiar to it from none other than actual being. It is this being
that has constructed it with passionate care, as if the flames of love that
gave it birth had stripped it of all its functional servitudes, reestablished
its original power, and restored its original poverties. (*Siloë,* 38)

Rather than the continuity of life, it is the discontinuity of birth
that ultimately needs to be explained. It is at the moment of birth that
one can measure the true power of being. This power is, as we shall see,
the return to the liberty of the possible, to those multiple resonances
born from the solitude of being.

But the force of this claim will become more apparent once we
have developed our metaphysical theory of habit by applying the themes
of discontinuous time.

II

In the interest of clarity, let us formulate our thesis by contrasting it up-
front with the theses of realism. Habit is ordinarily said to be *inscribed in
being.* We believe it would be better to say, invoking the jargon of geom-
eters, that habit is *exscribed to being.*[8]

The individual being, insofar as it is complex, corresponds first of
all to a simultaneity of instantaneous actions. It rediscovers itself only
to the degree that it resumes these simultaneous actions. We might say
that an individual, considered as the sum of its qualities and of its becoming, corresponds to a harmony of temporal rhythms. It is indeed
through *rhythm* that the continuity of the discontinuous will best be understood—a discontinuous continuity we must now establish in order to
interconnect the summits of being and to outline its unity. Rhythm traverses silence in the same way that being traverses the temporal vacuum
that separates instants. Being continues itself by habit, much as time
endures by the regular density of instants without duration. This is the
sense, at least, in which we interpret the Roupnelian thesis:

> The individual is the expression not of a constant cause but of a juxta-position of incessant memories held together by matter, whose ligature is itself but a habit overlapping all others. Being is no more than a strange site of memories; and one could almost say that the perma-nence with which it believes itself to be endowed is but the expression of habit to itself. (*Siloë*, 36)

Ultimately, the coherence of being is constituted neither by the in-herence of qualities nor by its material becoming. It is purely harmonic and aerial. It is fragile and free like a symphony. A particular habit is a sustained rhythm, where all acts repeat themselves while equalizing their novelty value with enough accuracy, yet without ever losing that domi-nant characteristic of being a novelty. The dilution of the new could be such that habit may at times pass for unconscious. Consciousness—so in-tense in the first attempt—seems to become dissipated as it shares itself among its multiple reiterations. But novelty organizes itself by economiz-ing itself. It invents in time, rather than inventing in space.

Life already finds its formal rule within temporal regulation. An organ, for instance, is shaped by its function. For organs to become complex, it suffices that these functions be active and frequent. It all comes down to using a growing number of instants offered by time. The atom that uses the greatest number of instants, it seems, develops habits so solid, so durable, so regular that we eventually come to take these habits as properties. Characteristics formed by well-utilized time, by well-ordered instants, thus appear to us as attributes of a substance. Let no one be astonished, then, to find formulas in *Siloë* that appear obscure to whomever resists recognizing that what we learn from examining our conscious life applies down the scale of being, all the way to matter itself:

> The work of elapsed Time remains wholly vigilant within the power and immobility of elements, and it is everywhere affirmed by the evi-dence that permeates the silence and composes the attention of things. (*Siloë*, 101)

In Roupnel's view, as in ours, it is indeed things themselves that pay the most attention to *Being*. And it is their attentiveness in seizing all of time's instants that gives rise to their permanence. Thus, matter is the most uniformly realized *habit of being*, for it is formed at the very level of the succession of instants.

But let us return to the point of departure of the psychological habit, for therein lies the source of our lesson. Given that rhythm-habits (which compose the life of mind as they do the life of matter) play them-selves out in a range of multiple registers, we are left with the impres-

sion that beneath every ephemeral habit there lies a more stable habit.
Clearly, then, the portrayal of an individual must take into account a
hierarchy of habits. We are easily tempted, therefore, to postulate a fundamental habit that would correspond to that simple, most unified and
monotonous habit of being—a fundamental habit that would constitute
the unity and identity of the individual. Seized by consciousness, such a
habit would constitute, for instance, the feeling of duration. But we believe it necessary to safeguard all the possibilities of interpretation ten-
dered by Roupnel's intuition. It does not seem to us that the individual
is as markedly defined as academic philosophy might assert: we should
speak neither of the unity nor of the identity of the self beyond the
synthesis realized by the *instant*. The problems of contemporary physics
even lead us to believe that it is equally dangerous to speak of the unity
or identity of a particular atom. The individual being, at whatever level it
is grasped—within matter, within life, or within thought—is a fairly variable sum of untallied habits. Since not all of the habits that characterize
that being—if they were known—benefit equally from all the instants
that might actualize them, its unity seems forever touched by contin-
gency. The individual is essentially nothing but a sum of accidents and,
what is more, that sum is itself accidental. At the same time, the being's
identity is never fully realized; it suffers from the fact that its wealth of
habits has not been managed with sufficient attention. Its global identity
is thus composed of more or less accurate repetitions, more or less detailed reflections. The individual will no doubt make an effort to trace its
today upon its yesterday, and this copy will be aided by the dynamics of
rhythms. But these rhythms have not all reached the same point in their
evolution, and that is how the most solid spiritual permanence—namely,
the affirmation of character and its desired identity—tends to degrade
into mere resemblance. Life henceforth carries our image from mirror
to mirror. We thus become reflections of reflections,[9] and our fortitude
is constituted by no more than a memory of our decision. Still, no matter how stable and resolute we are, we never keep ourselves completely
whole, for we have never been fully aware of our being in its entirety.

Furthermore, one might hesitate as to how best to interpret a hierarchy. Is true power to be found in clear resolve or in blind obedience?
This is why we ultimately resist the temptation to locate dominant habits
among the most unconscious ones. The conception of an individual as
an integral sum of rhythms lends itself, rather, to a decreasingly substan-
tialist interpretation—one that is increasingly removed from matter and
closer to conscious thought. To pose the question in musical terms: What
is it that brings about harmony and truly grants it movement? Is it the
melody, or is it the accompaniment? Shouldn't the force of evolution
be attributed to the most melodious score? Setting metaphors aside, let

us just say: it is *thought* that leads being. Beings transmit their heritage through vague or clear thought, through what is understood and especially through what is willed in the unity and innocence of the act. Thus every individual and complex being endures to the degree that it constitutes itself as a consciousness, to the degree that its will harmonizes with subordinate forces and finds this scheme of economic outflow, which is a habit. Our arteries bear the age of our habits.

It is in this roundabout way that a finalistic quality comes to enrich the notion of habit.[10] Roupnel does not provide a place for finality, in fact, without first surrounding himself with the most meticulous precautions. It would be evidently out of line to grant the future a force of real solicitation in a thesis that refuses to grant the past a real force of causality.

But if we are willing to come to terms with Roupnel's key intuition and follow him in placing temporal conditions on the same level as spatial conditions (even while the majority of philosophies attribute an unjustified explanatory privilege to space), we will notice numerous problems suddenly appearing under a more favorable light. Such is the case of "finalism."[11] It is striking indeed to note that in the world of matter *every privileged direction ultimately constitutes a privilege of propagation.* Thus we can argue that if an event propagates itself most rapidly along one crystal axis, this means that more instants are being utilized along that axis than in any other direction. In the same way, if life accepts the affirmation of instants following a specific cadence, it grows more rapidly in one specific direction. It appears as a linear succession of cells, for it is the summary of the propagation of a highly homogeneous generative force. A nerve or muscle fiber is a materialized habit, made up of well-chosen instants, strongly bonded together by a rhythm. Hence, as we stand before the tremendous wealth of choices offered by discontinuous instants linked by habits, we realize that it is possible to speak of *chronotropisms* corresponding to the various rhythms that constitute the living being.

This is how, from a Roupnelian perspective, we interpret the multiplicity of durations recognized by Bergson. Evoking rhythm, Bergson himself composes a metaphor when he writes:

> There is no single rhythm of duration. It is possible to imagine many different rhythms, slower or faster, which measure the degree of tension or relaxation of different kinds of consciousness and, thereby, fix their respective places within the scale of beings.[12]

We make the very same claim, of course, but in straightforward language that we believe translates reality more directly. We have in effect attributed reality to the instant and, in our view, it is the concatenation of instants that naturally forms the temporal rhythm. Since for Bergson the instant is nothing but an abstraction, it is with intervals of "unequal elasticity" that we would have to compose metaphoric rhythms. The multiplicity of durations is rightly mentioned, yet it is not explained by his thesis of temporal elasticity. Once again, the task of setting a threaded course upon the rough canvas of instants—a regular enough course to give the impression of being's continuity and the speed of becoming—falls upon consciousness. As we intend to show at a later point, it is in orienting our consciousness toward a more or less rational project that we will truly find the fundamental temporal coherence that corresponds to the simple habit of being.

This unexpected freedom of choice among possible creative instants and the flexibility in their links through distinct rhythms, present two strong arguments to help us understand the overlap in the development of diverse living species. We have long been struck by the fact that different animal species are coordinated historically as well as functionally. The succession of species displays the order of coexisting organs within one particular individual. Natural science is, at our pleasure, a matter of history or description: time is the schema that mobilizes it, and finalistic coordination is the schema that describes it most clearly. Within one particular being, in other words, the coordination of functions and the finalism of functions are two reciprocal aspects of one same fact. The order of becoming is simultaneously the becoming of an order. That which is coordinated within the species is subordinated within time, and vice versa. A habit is a certain order of instants chosen from the basic ensemble of moments in time; it plays itself out at a specific pitch and with a distinct tone. It is a set of habits, then, that makes it possible for us to continue being amid the multiplicity of our attributes, leaving us under the impression of having been, even though all we could ever find as the substantial source of our being is the reality granted us by the present instant. Likewise, it is because habit is itself a perspective of acts that we can posit ends and goals for our future.

Habit's invitation to follow the rhythm of well-ordered acts is ultimately experienced as an imperative of a quasi-rational and aesthetic nature. What compels us to persevere in being is then not so much a set of forces as it is a set of reasons. It is this rational and aesthetic coherence in the superior rhythms of thought that constitutes the keystone of being.

Such ideal unity brings to Roupnel's often-bitter philosophy just that touch of rational optimism—measured and courageous—that turns his book toward broader moral concerns. We are thus led to examine, in a new chapter, the idea of progress in connection with the thesis of discontinuous time.

3

The Idea of Progress and the Intuition of Discontinuous Time

If . . . the being I love most in the world came and asked me one day what choice he should make—what refuge is the most profound, the sweetest, the most immune to attack—I would advise him to shelter his destiny in the haven of a soul devoted to noble growth.
—Maeterlinck, *Sagesse et destinée*, 1902

I

An apparent difficulty still lingers in Roupnel's theory of habit—a conundrum we will now attempt to resolve. It is in the natural course of this effort at clarification that we will be led to derive a metaphysics of progress from the intuitions of *Siloë*.

The difficulty is the following: in order to penetrate the full meaning of the *idea of habit*, we must associate two concepts that appear at first glance to contradict each other: *repetition* and *origination*. If, however, we are willing to see that every particular habit is dependent upon a more general habit—the clear and conscious habit of will—this objection is bound to dissolve.[1] We thus prefer to define habit in its full sense through a formula that reconciles two concepts often prematurely opposed by criticism: habit is the will to *begin* to *repeat* oneself.

If Roupnel's theory is correctly understood, we need not take habit as a mechanism deprived of innovative action. There would be a contradiction in terms if we said that habit is a passive power. The repetition that characterizes habit is a repetition that restructures even as it rediscovers itself.

Maurice Maeterlinck, *Sagesse et destinée* (Paris: Bibliothèque-Charpentier, 1902), §37, 90–91. All translations of *Sagesse et destinée* are mine.

Being is moreover governed not so much by necessary conditions to subsist as by sufficient conditions to progress. A just measure of novelty is needed in order to arouse being. Samuel Butler puts it well:

> The introduction of slightly new elements into our manner is attended with benefit; the new can be fused with the old, and the monotony of our action is relieved. But if the new element is too foreign, we cannot fuse the old and new—nature seeming equally to hate too wide a deviation from our ordinary practice, and no deviation at all. (*Life and Habit*, 166)

It is in this way that habit becomes progress. We must hence *desire* progress in order to preserve the efficacy of habit. What determines the true value of the initial instant that launches the habit in every one of its recurrences is this very desire for progress.

Roupnel had no doubt entertained the idea of the *eternal return*. But he immediately understood that this true and fertile idea could not be an absolute. In being reborn we heighten life:

> We do not come back to life in vain! . . . A new beginning is not constituted by an eternal always, ever identical with itself! . . . Our cerebral acts, our thoughts, are resumed in keeping with the ritual of increasingly acquired habits, becoming invested with endlessly accrued physical loyalties! If our faults aggravate their fatal contours, sharpening and worsening their forms and effects . . . our useful and beneficial acts also fill the path of everlasting steps with stronger and steadier footprints. Some new resolution enters the act with each new beginning and, through its results, gradually begets an unprecedented abundance. Let us not say that the act is permanent: it unceasingly builds upon the precision of its origins and its effects. We live each new life as a passing project: but life bequeaths life with all its fresh imprints. The act reviews its intentions and consequences with increasing rigor, thereby fulfilling what can never be finished. And generosity grows in our works and multiplies within us! . . . Whoever saw us in ancient days dragging a primitive soul—piteous mire and sensual clay—across the earth, would they recognize us under the great winds of spirit? . . . We come from afar with our warm blood . . . and here we are, the winged Soul, the Thought in the Storm! (*Siloë*, 186)

So protracted a destiny proves that, by perpetually returning to the sources of being, we have found the courage of renewed flight. Rather than a doctrine of the *eternal return*, Roupnel's thesis thus offers us a doctrine of the *eternal reprise*. It represents the continuity of courage within the discontinuity of attempts, the continuity of the ideal despite the rupture of facts. Every time Bergson speaks of continuity that prolongs itself[2] (continuity of our inner life, continuity of a voluntary movement), we can translate his claim by saying that it is a matter of a discontinuous form reconstituting itself. Every effective prolongation is an addition. All identity is resemblance.

We recognize ourselves in our character because we imitate ourselves, and because our personality is thus the habit of our own name. It is because we unify ourselves around our name and dignity—the nobility of the poor—that we can transport the integrity of a soul into the future. Besides, the copy we constantly remake must also be improved upon or else the useless model is tarnished, and the soul, which is essentially an aesthetic determination, dissolves.

Born and reborn, beginning or beginning anew—it is always, for the monad, the same action that is attempted. But occasions are not always the same. Not all resumptions are synchronous; not all instants are utilized and relinked by the same rhythms. Since occasions are nothing but shadows of conditions, all strength resides within the heart of instants that give new birth to being and recapture the task that has begun. An essential novelty in the form of freedom manifests itself in these resumptions; and so it is that habit—through the renewal of discontinuous time—can become progress in every sense of the term.

Habit theory thus becomes reconciled in Roupnel with a negation of the physical and material effect of the past. Although the past may indeed persist, we believe it survives only as a truth, only as a rational value, only as an ensemble of harmonious solicitations toward progress. The past is an easy domain to actualize, if you will, but it is actualized only to the degree that it has been successful. Progress is hence assured by the permanence of logical and aesthetic conditions.

This historian's philosophy of life is made even clearer by his admission of the uselessness of history itself, or history as a sum of facts. Certainly, there are historical forces that can come to life again, but for this to happen they must receive the synthesis of the instant and capture "the vigor of short cuts"—the dynamics of rhythms, as we would say. Roupnel himself of course does not distinguish between a philosophy of history and a philosophy of life. Here again, the present dominates all. As seen when he writes on the genesis of species:

> The types that have survived have done so in proportion not to their historical role, but to their present role. Only remotely can embryonic forms still recall specific forms adapted to ancient conditions of historical life. The adaptation that once realized them no longer has pres-

ent claims. They are, if you will, adaptations of forms in disuse. They are but the spoils seized by an abductor, for they are forms of past types placed in the service of another. Their active interdependence replaces their abolished independence. They have value only to the degree they call upon one another. (*Siloë*, 55)

Thus, we again find that present harmony takes precedence over a pre-established harmony which, in Leibniz's theory, would load the past with the weight of destiny.

The most solid and coherent reasons for enriching being are, ultimately, the conditions of progress. And Roupnel summarizes his point of view in a formula which is all the more significant in that it is articulated in the section of the book devoted to an examination of biological theses: "Assimilation progresses in proportion to the progress of reproduction" (*Siloë*, 74). What persists is always what regenerates itself.

II

Roupnel was naturally aware of the extent to which the psychological aspect of habit facilitates progress. As he aptly put it:

> The idea of progress is logically associated with the idea of new beginnings and of repetition. Habit, as such, already signifies a kind of progress. Through the effect of acquired habit, an act that begins again does so with more speed and precision. The gestures that carry it out shed their excessive dimensions and useless complication; they simplify and abridge themselves. Parasitic movements disappear. The act reduces outlay and waste to a strict, necessary minimum—both in terms of energy and time. As dynamism is improved and refined, so are the work and result simultaneously perfected. (*Siloë*, 157)

These remarks are so classical that Roupnel need not insist upon them. But he does admit that their application to the theory of being's instantaneity bears some difficulties. In essence, the problem of assuring progress over and above a past demonstrated to be ineffective is the same as the problem we encountered when attempting to establish the roots of habit within that same past. It is necessary, therefore, to return to the same point time and again, and to struggle against the false clarity of the efficacy of an abolished past, the postulate of our opponents. Roupnel's position is particularly candid. In postulating this efficacy, he says:

We are the constant dupes of a pervasive illusion that makes us believe in the reality of objective time, leading us to accept its presumed effects. In the life of being, two successive instants have, between them, the independence that corresponds to the independence of the two molecular rhythms they interpret. This independence, of which we take no notice when it is a matter of two consecutive situations, becomes manifest as soon as we consider phenomena not immediately consecutive to each other. But then we claim to attribute the indifference between them to the duration that sets them apart. In reality, it is only when we come to recognize the dissolving energy and separating virtue of duration that we begin to render justice to its negative nature and potential nothingness. Whether taken in strong or weak doses, duration is never more than an illusion. And the power of its nothingness separates the least consecutive phenomena in appearance just as it does the least contemporaneous.

Thus, between consecutive phenomena, there is passivity and indifference. The real dependence, as we have shown, is composed of symmetries and references among homologous situations. It is on the basis of such symmetries and references that energy sculpts its acts and molds its gestures. Real clusters of instants would therefore be related to true links among the situations of being. If we wished to construct a continuous duration at all costs, it would always be a subjective duration whose lived instants referred to the homologous series in it. (*Siloë*, 158)

One more step, and—having started from that homology or that symmetry of grouped instants—we will arrive at the idea that duration, always indirectly grasped, has no force other than that of its creative progress.

[Such progress] is a matter of improvement—a subtle improvement no doubt, but one that is logically undeniable and quite sufficient to introduce differentiation among instants and, hence, to introduce the element of duration. We thus realize that such duration is nothing other than the expression of a dynamic progress. And now we, who have referred everything back to dynamism, will conclude quite simply that continuous duration, if it exists, is the expression of progress. (*Siloë*, 158)

A scale of perfection can thus be applied directly to the group of instants gathered via active chronotropisms. Through a strange reversal [*réciproque*],[3] it is because there is *progress* in the aesthetic, moral, or religious sense that we can be certain of the march of time. Instants are distinct because they are fertile. And they are fertile not by virtue of the memories they can actualize, but by the fact that a temporal novelty is added at that point, a temporal novelty suitably adapted to the rhythm of progress.

But it is perhaps with regard to the simplest or the most simplified problems that this equation between pure duration and progress will be most readily recognized. For the need to articulate time's essential value of renewal will become all the more evident in such cases. Time endures only through invention.

In order to simplify the temporal element, Bergson also starts out with a melody. But instead of highlighting the fact that a melody has meaning only through the diversity of its sounds, and instead of recognizing that each sound itself has a varied life, Bergson tries to show that by eliminating this diversity between sounds, and within a single sound, we can ultimately reach uniformity. By removing discernible matter from sound, in other words, he expects to find the uniformity of fundamental time. In our view, only the uniformity of nothingness could be attained this way. If we examine a sound that is objectively as plain and simple as can be, we will notice that this simple sound is never subjectively uniform. It is impossible to maintain any kind of synchronism between the rhythm of the stimulus and the rhythm of sensation. Even the most cursory acoustic experiment will help us recognize that our perception of sound is not a simple summation: vibrations cannot each play an identical role since they do not open and fill the same space. One proof of this is that a sound prolonged without variation becomes increasingly agonizing, as Octave Mirbeau once keenly noted.[4] The same case against uniformity could be made in every field, for pure and simple repetition has similar effects in both the organic and the inorganic world. Such repetition, when it is too uniform, becomes a principle of rupture for matter. Even the hardest material, when subjected to certain monotonous rhythms, is bound to disintegrate. When all it takes is to prolong the purest sound for its character to change, how can we expect to advance the psychological study of acoustic sensation by endorsing Bergson's postulates about "the continuation of what precedes in what follows," "uninterrupted transition, multiplicity without diversity,"[5] and "succession without separation"? Even without taking into account the sound that becomes painful through persistent prolongation, we should recognize that by just allowing a sound its full musical value in a measured prolongation, the sound renews itself and sings! The closer attention we pay to an apparently uniform sensation, the more it diversifies itself. We would truly be victims of reductive abstraction if we imagined a meditation that simplified sense data. Sensation is variety. Memory alone confers uniformity.

Between Bergson's method and our own, therefore, the selfsame difference persists: Bergson takes eventful time at the very level of the consciousness of events, and gradually obliterates those events, or the consciousness of events, until he reaches what he believes to be event-free time—namely, the consciousness of pure duration. By contrast, the only way we ourselves can feel time is by multiplying conscious instants. Should laziness slacken our meditation, enough instants enriched by the sentient life of the flesh may still remain viable, allowing us to retain the more or less vague feeling that we endure. But if we wish to shed light on this feeling, the only way to do so is through a multiplication of thoughts. Consciousness of time is always, for us, an awareness of the utilization of *instants*—it is always active, never passive. In short, consciousness of our duration is consciousness of the *progress* of our innermost being, whether this progress is real, a simulation, or simply a dream. Complexity thus organized into progress becomes clearer and simpler, while the rhythm properly renewed becomes more coherent than pure and simple repetition. Furthermore, if—through informed organization—we do attain uniformity in our meditation, such uniformity will amount to a new conquest in our view, for it is found through an ordering of creative instants, as in one of those general and fertile thoughts capable of embracing and commanding a thousand ordered thoughts. Duration is therefore richness, for it cannot be revealed through abstraction. We weave the fabric of duration by placing concrete instants one after the other (again, without touching one another)—each instant rich in conscious and well-measured novelty. The coherence of duration is the coordination of a method of enrichment. We cannot speak of pure and simple uniformity unless it is in reference to a world of abstractions, to an account of nothingness. It is not through the path of reductive simplicity that we must reach the limits of experience, but rather through the path of richness.

The only truly uniform duration is, in our view, a uniformly varied duration, a progressive duration.

III

If we were asked to assign a traditional philosophical label to Roupnel's doctrine of time, at this point, we would say that his doctrine corresponds to one of the clearest cases of phenomenalism [*phénoménisme*]. To say that for Roupnel time counts as nothing but substance would be definitely to mischaracterize it, for in *Siloë* time is always taken at once as substance and as attribute. Then that curious trinity without substance, which allows for *duration, habit,* and *progress* to be perpetually exchanging their effects, becomes understandable.[6] From the moment we grasp that perfect equation of the three fundamental phenomena of becoming, we realize it would be unfair to raise the objection of a vicious circle in this case. Were we to start out from common intuitions, critics would surely object that duration cannot explain progress since progress demands duration in order to develop, and that habit cannot actualize the past since being does not have the means to preserve an inactive past. But discursive order does not prove anything against the intuitive unity that vividly takes shape when one meditates on *Siloë.* It is not a matter of classifying realities, but of making phenomena understood by reconstructing them in multiple ways. There is but one reality: the instant. Duration, habit, and progress are only groupings of instants—the simplest among the phenomena of time. None of these temporal phenomena can have an ontological privilege. We are thus free to read their connection in both directions, to traverse the circle that relinks them in either way.

The metaphysical synthesis of progress and duration leads Roupnel, toward the end of his book, to guarantee ultimate perfection by inscribing it at the very heart of the divinity that grants us time. For a long time, Roupnel has subsisted as a soul in waiting, a soul in hopeful expectation. But from this very waiting he appears to have garnered wisdom. In a formula, striking for its intellectual humility, he notes that the transcendence of God molds itself to the immanence of our desire: "The unknowable is no longer beyond our reach when we perceive at least the form wherein it conceals itself, if not the cause which explains it" (*Siloë,* 172). Our desires, our very hopes, and our love would thus trace out for us the external contours of the Supreme Being.

   Light then traverses from reason to the heart: "Love! What other word could offer a verbal envelope adapted from our spiritual nature to the intimate harmony that constitutes the nature of things, to the grand and solemn rhythm that brings the entire Universe to fruition?" (*Siloë,* 162). Yes, for instants to yield duration, for duration to yield progress, Love must be inscribed upon the very foundations of Time . . . Reading these loving pages, we sense the poet once again on the way toward the intimate and mysterious source of his own Siloam . . .

   To each his own path. Since we have allowed ourselves to draw from Roupnel's book that which best aids our own mind and spirit, let us point out that it is in seeking the rational character of Love that we pursue our dream.

   The ways of intimate progress are, for us, the ways of logic and general laws. The great memories of a soul, those which grant a soul its meaning and depth—we realize one day—are on their way to becoming *rational*. Only a being for whom there is reason to mourn can be mourned for long. Then it is stoic reason that consoles the heart, without requiring it to forget. In Love itself what is special is always small— it remains unusual and isolated: it finds no place within the normal rhythm that shapes sentimental habit. We can place all the particularities we desire around our memories of Love—the hawthorn hedge or the flowery front gate, the autumn evening or the springtime dawn. Still the true heart remains constant. Though the scene may change, the actor is always the same. In its essential novelty, the joy of loving can surprise and marvel. But to experience love in its depth is to live it in its simplicity. The paths of sadness are no less regular. When a love has lost its mystery by losing its future, when destiny brings reading to an end by brutally closing the book, we find within memory, beneath all the variations of regret, the theme of human suffering—so clear, so simple, so general. At the edge of a grave, Guyau was still saying in a philosophical verse:

"The sweetest happiness is the one we hope for."

To which we respond by evoking

The purest happiness, the one we have lost.

Our opinion, clearly that of a philosopher, will no doubt be countered by the extensive experience of novelists. But we cannot avoid the impression that the richness of individual characters, often heteroclite, places the novel within an atmosphere of naive and facile realism that is ultimately but a form of primitive psychology. From our point of view, on the other hand, passion is all the more varied in its effects the simpler and more logical its principles. A fantasy never enjoys enough duration to fulfill all the possibilities of an affective being. It is but a stray possibility, an ephemeral attempt at best, a rhythm out of breath. A deep love, on the other hand, is a harmonization of all the possibilities of being, for it is essentially a reference to being, an ideal of temporal harmony where the present is endlessly devoted to preparing a future. It is at once duration, habit, and progress.

To strengthen the heart, we need to reinforce passion with morality, to discover the general reasons for loving. Only then can we understand the metaphysical import of theories that seek the very force of temporal coordination in sympathy and care. It is because we love and suffer that time prolongs itself in us, and endures. Half a century before today's celebrated theses,[7] Guyau had already recognized that "deep down, memory and sympathy have . . . the same origin" (Genèse, 80). He had demonstrated that time is essentially affective:

> The idea of past and future is not only the necessary condition for all mental anguish; it is, from a certain point of view, the very principle of moral suffering. (Genèse, 82)

We forge our time, as we do our space, through the simple care we take in relation to our future, and through our desire for our own expansion. This is how our being—heart and reason—corresponds to the universe and calls for eternity. As Roupnel once said in a remark we reproduce here in its original version:

> Therein resides the very genius of our soul—in yearning for end-less space, hungering for boundless duration, thirsting for the Ideal, hounded by the Infinite whose life is the disquiet of a perpetual else-where and its nature but the protracted agony of an expansion to the entire Universe.[8]

We are thus engaged in the paths of the universal and the permanent by the very fact that we live, by the very fact that we love and suffer. If our love languishes at times without strength, it is largely because we are victims of the realism of our passion. We attach our love to our name, whereas it is the general truth of a soul. We do not want to bind the diversity of our desires into a coherent and rational whole, even though they have no efficacy unless they each complete and complement one another. If we but had the wisdom to listen to the harmony of the possible within ourselves, we would recognize that the myriad rhythms of instants come to us bearing realities so precisely interrelated that we should understand the ultimately rational character of the pains and joys that reside at the source of being. Suffering is always linked to redemption, joy always linked to an intellectual effort. Everything doubles up in mutual reinforcement within ourselves when we are willing to grasp all the possibilities of duration. In Maeterlinck's words:

> If you love, it is not the beloved who will shape your destiny. What will transform your life is the knowledge of self you will have discovered in the depths of this love. And if you have been betrayed, it is not the betrayal that matters. It is the forgiveness it has engendered in your soul—the more or less general, the more or less elevated and reflective nature of this forgiveness—that will turn your existence toward the clear and peaceful limits of your destiny, where you will see yourself better than

if others had remained forever faithful to you. But if betrayal has not
increased the simplicity, highest faith, and extent of your love, you will
have been betrayed in vain, and you will be able to tell yourself that
nothing has come of it. (*Sagesse et Destinée,* §9, 27)

How better to say that being can preserve from the past only what
serves its own progress, only what is able to enter into a rational system
of sympathy and affection. Nothing endures unless it has reasons to endure. Duration is thus the first phenomenon of the principle of *sufficient*
reason for the binding of instants. In other words, there is but one principle of continuity within the forces of the world—namely, the permanence of rational conditions, the conditions of moral and aesthetic success. Those conditions command the heart as they do the mind. It is they
that determine the solidarity of instants in progress.

Intimate duration is always a matter of wisdom. What coordinates
the world is not the force of the past. It is the harmony, always in tension,
that the world is poised to realize. One might speak of a "preestablished
harmony," but it cannot merely be a matter of a preestablished harmony
in things. There is no effective action except through a preestablished
harmony in reason. The force of time is wholly condensed within that
novel instant where sight awakens, near the fountain of Siloam, touched
by a divine redeemer who in one gesture grants us joy and reason, and
the way to eternal being through truth and goodness.

Conclusion

Beings devoted to reason find their strength in solitude. Within themselves they have the means for renewal. The eternity of truth lies at
their disposal without the burden and custody of past experience. Jean
Guéhenno was right to say: "Reason, this stranger without memory and
without heritage, forever bent on recommencing everything" (*Caliban
parle*),[1] for it is truly through reason that everything can begin again.
Failure is but a negative proof, failure is always experimental. Within the
domain of reason, it is enough to bring two obscure themes together for
the clarity of evidence to strike. A fertile novelty is thus brought forth
from an old misunderstanding. If there is an eternal return that sustains
the world, it is the eternal return of reason.

   Not from the side of such rational innocence, however, does Roupnel seek the paths to the redemption of being. It is within Art that he
finds a means most directly adapted to the very principles of creation. In
pages that go to the very heart of aesthetic intuition, he restores for us
this freshness of soul and the senses that renews the poetic force.

> It is Art that liberates us from literary and artistic routine . . . It cures
> the soul's social fatigue and rejuvenates worn-out perception. It restores
> vitality and realistic representation to forms of degraded expression.
> It brings truth back to sensation, honesty back to emotion. It teaches
> us to use our senses and our souls as if nothing had yet deprived them
> of vigor or stained their clairvoyance. It teaches us to see and listen
> to the Universe as if we were just now enjoying its sound and sudden
> revelation. It restores to our gaze the grace of an awakening Nature. It
> bestows on us the enchanting hours of primitive mornings streaming
> with novel creations. It turns us into that being filled with wonder who
> heard the voices of Nature being born, who was present at the emer-
> gence of the firmament, and before whom the Sky arose as a Stranger.
> (*Siloë*, 196)

   But again if art is solitude, like reason, we soon discover that solitude is art itself. After suffering we are delivered "to the sublime solitude
of our heart . . . whereupon our soul, having broken its infamous chains,
returns to its shrouded temple." And Roupnel continues:

Art listens to this inner voice. It brings us the hidden murmur. It is the voice of supernatural conscience that oversees the inalienable and perpetual reserves within us. Art restores us to the primordial site of our being, to that immense point where we inhabit the entire Universe. Our miserable little parcel here assumes its universal quality, and through it reveals to us the authority of Art. Triumphant over all the discontinuous themes that divide Being and make up the individual, Art is the sense of Harmony that restores us to the World's gentle rhythm and returns us to the Infinity that summons us.

Everything in us then becomes a participant in this absolute rhythm wherein the whole phenomenon of the World unfolds. Then, everything in us regulates itself in terms of supreme directives, everything becomes clarified in terms of intimate clairvoyant insights. Lights take on their message-giving sense. Lines unfold the grace of a mysterious association with infinite harmonies. Sounds develop their melody within an inner path where the entire Universe sings. A vehement love, a universal sympathy searches our hearts and seeks to bind us to the soul that trembles in all things.

The Universe that assumes its beauty is the Universe that assumes its meaning; and the outdated images we project upon it fall from the absolute face that emerges from the mystery. (*Siloë,* 198)

At the root of this contemplative redemption, we believe, lies a force that enables us to accept life in a single act with all its intimate contradictions. In placing absolute nothingness at both edges of the instant, Roupnel must have been led to such intensity of consciousness that the entire image of a destiny was legible, in a sudden glimmer, within the very act of mind and spirit. The profound cause of Roupnelian melancholy can perhaps be traced to this metaphysical necessity: we must hold both regret and hope within one and the same thought. A felt synthesis of contraries: such is the lived instant.

We are moreover capable of reversing the affective axis of time, placing hope within a memory into which freshness has been restored through our reverie. On the other hand, we might well be discouraged by contemplating the future for, at certain times—at the peak of maturity, for instance—we realize that we can no longer postpone the custody of our hopes until tomorrow. The bitterness of life is the regret of not being able to hope, of no longer being able to hear the rhythms that beckon us to play our part in the symphony of becoming. It is then that the "smiling regret"[2] advises us to invite death and to welcome the monotonous rhythms of matter, like a lullaby.

This is the metaphysical atmosphere in which we like to place *Siloë*. It is with this personal interpretation that we like to reread this strange work. It speaks to us in power and in sadness, for it is both truth and courage. In this bitter and tender work, good cheer is indeed always a conquest. Goodness systematically transcends the consciousness of evil, for the consciousness of evil is already the desire for redemption. Optimism is will, even though pessimism is clear knowledge. Astonishing privilege of intimacy! It is truly the human heart that is the greatest power of coherence in the face of conflicting ideas. While reading *Siloë*, we were keenly aware that we were contributing, by our own commentary, an assortment of loaded contradictions. But sympathy with the work soon encouraged us to trust the lessons we drew from our own errors.

This is why *Siloë* is a beautiful human book. It does not teach; it evokes. A work of solitude, it calls for solitary reading. One finds the book as one finds oneself when reentering into oneself. If you contradict it, it responds to you. If you follow it, it incites you. The book is hardly closed, when already the desire to reopen it is reborn; hardly silenced, when already an echo awakens in the soul who understood it.

"Poetic Instant and Metaphysical Instant" by Gaston Bachelard

I

Poetry is instant metaphysics. In a short poem it must deliver, all at once, the vision of a universe and the secret of a soul—an insight into being and objects. If it only follows the time of life, it is less than life. It cannot be more than life unless it immobilizes life, evoking on the spot the dialectic of joy and suffering. It is thus the principle of an essential simultaneity in which the most scattered and disjointed being attains its unity.

While the way to every other metaphysical experience is prepared by endless prologues, poetry rejects preambles, principles, methods, and proofs. It rejects doubt. At most, it calls for a prelude of silence. By first knocking upon hollow words, poetry hushes the din of prose or the lingering echoes that would leave a continuous trail of thoughts and murmurs in the reader's soul. Then, in the wake of these empty sonorities, it yields its instant. It is in order to give rise to a complex instant, brimming with simultaneities, that a poet shatters the simple continuity of shackled time.

Every true poem can reveal the elements of suspended time, meterless time—a time we shall call *vertical* in order to distinguish it from everyday time, which sweeps along horizontally with the streaming waters and the blowing winds. Hence the paradox to be plainly stated: whereas prosodic time is horizontal, poetic time is vertical. The role of prosody is to organize successive sounds; it conducts cadences, orchestrating fervent passions and tensions—often, alas, on the offbeat. By accepting the consequences of a poetic instant, prosody allows its reinsertion into prose, explanatory thought, love stories, social life, ordinary life—sleek, linear, continuous life. Yet all the rules of prosody are but means, worn-out means. The aim is *verticality* as depth or height—it is that stabilized

Originally published in the French review *Messages: Métaphysique et poésie* 2 (1939) and later in *L'Arc* (1961), this text supplements Bachelard's meditations on the problem of time in the *Intuition of the Instant*.

instant wherein simultaneities prove, by ordering themselves, that the poetic instant has metaphysical scope.[1]

The poetic instant is thus necessarily complex: it moves, it proves— it invites, it consoles—it is astonishing and familiar. It is essentially a harmonic relation between two opposites. Within a poet's passionate instant, there is always a touch of reason; within the reasoned rejection, always a touch of passion. Successive antitheses already fill a poet with pleasure. But for these antitheses to yield an experience of rapture and ecstasy, they must contract into ambivalence. Only then does a poetic instant arise . . . At the very least, a poetic instant is the awareness of an ambivalence. But it is more than that, for it is a stimulated ambivalence—an active, dynamic ambivalence. The poetic instant compels us to value or devalue. Being rises or descends in a poetic instant without accepting world time, which would inevitably turn ambivalence back into antithesis, simultaneity into succession.

This affinity between antithesis and ambivalence can be easily verified if we are willing to commune with a poet who keenly experiences the two terms of his antitheses in one and the same instant. The second term is not evoked by the first. Both terms are born together. A poem's true poetic instants are hence to be found at all those points where the human heart is able to invert antitheses. More intuitively speaking, a well-knit ambivalence is revealed through its temporal character: instead of masculine, vigorous time which thrusts forth and conquers, instead of gentle, submissive time which weeps and regrets, we have the androgynous instant. The mystery of poetry is androgynous.

II

But is it possible to define time by this multitude of contradictory events enclosed within a single instant? Is time to be defined entirely by this vertical dimension that presides over the poetic instant? Yes, indeed, for such accumulated simultaneities are *ordered* simultaneities. They add a depth-dimension to the instant by granting it internal order. Now, time is order and nothing but order. And all order is time. Therefore, the order of ambivalences within the instant is time. And it is this vertical time that the poet discovers when he rejects horizontal time—namely, the becoming of others, the becoming of life, the becoming of the world. Let us then lay out the three orders of successive experience from which every being enchained within horizontal time must find release:

1. The social framework of duration—broken by learning not to refer one's own time to the time of others;

2. The phenomenal framework of duration—broken by learning not to refer one's own time to the time of things;

3. The vital framework of duration—broken by learning not to refer one's own time to the time of life (a hard exercise), by suspending concern over the beat of one's heart or the surge of delight.

Only then might one attain the auto-synchronous reference point at the center of oneself, stripped of all peripheral life. Flat horizontality suddenly vanishes. Time no longer flows. It spouts.

III

In order to retain or, rather, to recover this stabilized poetic instant, certain poets like Mallarmé will directly assault horizontal time by inverting syntax, thus detaining or deflecting the consequences of the poetic instant. Complex prosodies cast pebbles into streams, producing ripples and eddies that shatter futile images and erase reflections. Reading Mallarmé, we are often struck by a sense of recurrent time capable of rescuing bygone instants. We can then experience, belatedly, those instants which should have been lived: a feeling all the more remarkable as it is stripped of regret, repentance, or nostalgia. It is simply fashioned from *wrought time,* which manages on occasion to insert the echo before the voice, denial within avowal.

Other more fortunate poets seize the stabilized instant naturally. Baudelaire, like the Chinese, sees time [*l'heure*] in a cat's eye—that impassive hour where passion is so complete it disdains the very need to run its course: "In the depths of its charming eyes I can tell time distinctly—always that same solemn hour, vast as space, undivided into minutes or seconds—that motionless hour, unmarked by clocks. . ."[2] For poets who realize the instant with such ease, the poem does not unfold—it is knit, it is woven knot by knot. Their drama is not carried out. Their evil is a tranquil flower.[3]

Poised at the point of midnight, without heeding the breath of hours, the poet divests himself of all that is unnecessary in life, experiencing the abstract ambivalence of being and nonbeing. In the darkness, he is better able to seize his own light. Solitude grants him the boon of solitary thought—thought that rises undistracted, encountering peace in pure exaltation.

Vertical time rises. On occasion it plunges. Midnight, for those who know how to read Poe's "The Raven," no longer strikes horizontally. It strikes within the soul, sinking deeper and deeper . . . Rare is the night when I dare sink down to the very bottom, down to the twelfth stroke, to the twelfth wound, to the twelfth memory . . . All too soon I return to superficial time. I go on, enchained yet again as I reclaim my place in life among the living. We must keep betraying our ghosts, in order to live . . .

It is along the axis of vertical time—descending time—that our worst pains are piled up: pains without temporal causality, acute pains that relentlessly and pointlessly pierce the heart.

It is along the axis of vertical time—ascending time—that solace without hope gains strength—a strange and autochthonous solace that stands unaided. Briefly put, all that detaches us from cause or recompense, all that denies our private history, even desire itself—all that devalues both past and future, at one and the same time—is contained within the poetic instant.

To examine a tiny fragment of vertical time let us take, for example, Baudelaire's poetic instant of *smiling regret*—at the very moment when night subsides and darkness stabilizes, when the hours barely breathe and, already, solitude is remorse![4] The ambivalent poles of *smiling regret* almost touch. The slightest oscillation prompts them to exchange places. The *smiling regret* is thus one of the most sensitive ambivalences of a sensitive heart. Yet it develops most clearly within vertical time, for neither of its moments—smile or regret—precedes the other. Here, feeling is reversible or, to put it better, being's reversibility is *imbued with feeling:* a smile regrets and a regret smiles, the regret consoles. Neither time, articulated sequentially, causes the other—proof that they are poorly expressed in terms of consecutive time, horizontal time. A transformation occurs, nonetheless, from one to the other—a transformation that can only be experienced vertically as it yields the impression that regret lightens up, that a soul is lifted, that the ghost forgives. Here, indeed, misfortune flowers. Within the *smiling regret,* a sensitive metaphysician will hence discover the formal beauty of misfortune. It is in terms of formal causality that one can understand the value of volatilization that marks the poetic instant. This is new evidence that formal causality takes place within an instant, in vertical time, whereas efficient causality develops horizontally, in life and in things, by grouping together instants of varying intensities.

Naturally, it is also possible to experience longer-term ambivalences within the perspective of the instant: "When I was a child, my heart used to be haunted by two contradictory feelings: the horror of life, and the ecstasy of life."[5] Instants when these feelings are experienced *together* bring time to a standstill, for they are experienced as associated by an intense fascination for life. They abduct being from ordinary duration. Such ambivalence cannot be described in terms of consecutive time, as a common balance sheet of fleeting joys and pleasures. Contrasts as sharp and fundamental as that belong to a metaphysics of the immediate. Their oscillation is experienced in a single instant through states of ecstasy and depression that might even contradict events: disgust for life can overtake us in joy as fatally as can pride in misfortune. Cyclical temperaments, swept along by contradictory states in ordinary time that echo the phases of the moon, offer but parodies of fundamental ambivalence. Only an in-depth psychology of the instant could provide us with the necessary schemas for an understanding of the essential drama of poetry.

IV

It is moreover surprising that one of the poets to seize decisive instants most intensely should be the poet of *correspondences*. A Baudelairean correspondence is not, as often claimed, a simple transposition that would deliver a code of sensual analogies. It is the sum of sentient being in a single instant. But the sensory simultaneities that blend perfumes, colors, and sounds do no more than arouse the most remote and profound simultaneities. The dual eternity of good and evil is found within these two unities of night and light. And whatever "vastness" there might be within light and night should not suggest a spatial vision. Night and light are not evoked for the sake of their extension, their infinity, but for the sake of their unity. Night is not a space. It is a threat of eternity. Night and light are motionless instants—black or white, happy or sad, black and white, sad and happy instants. Never has a poetic instant been more complete than in the verse that allows us to experience, in one breath, the immensities of both day and night. Never has the ambivalence of feelings, the Manichaeism of principles, succeeded in making itself felt so deeply in the flesh.

Meditating along these lines, we come to the sudden conclusion that *all morality is instantaneous*. The categorical imperative of morality has nothing to do with duration. It does not retain any sensory cause; it anticipates no consequence. It steers a straight course, vertically, into the time of forms and persons.[6] The poet here becomes a natural guide for the metaphysician who seeks to understand all the powers of instantaneous connections, the fervor of sacrifice, without succumbing to the divisions of a crude philosophical duality of subject and object, nor being detained by the dualism of egotism and duty. The poet brings a subtler dialectic to life. He reveals at the same time, in a single instant, the solidarity of form and person. He proves that form is a person, and that a person is form. Poetry thus becomes an instant of formal causality, an instant of personal power. It loses interest in what merely shatters and dissipates, in a temporal duration that disperses echoes. It seeks the instant. It needs nothing but the instant. It creates the instant. Without the instant, there is only prose and singsong. It is in the vertical time of an immobilized instant that poetry finds its specific dynamism. Such pure dynamism belongs to pure poetry. It develops vertically within the time of forms and persons.

Reading Bachelard Reading *Siloë:* An Excerpt from "Introduction to Bachelard's Poetics" by Jean Lescure

The paradox of every great work, particularly every poetic work, is that it refers indefinitely both to itself and beyond itself. It appeals to two equally open-ended domains: (1) that of the reader's consciousness wherein the notions it suggests and inspires take root, in addition to those it overtly professes; and (2) one that foments the gradual development of a thought which, though momentarily arrested by the author's death, remains open to the dense network of multiple figures and combinations it sanctions indefinitely, perhaps because it has resisted any strict systematization while allowing itself instead to be defined by its encounter with what remains its future. Bachelard knew that the thought he strove to seize strikes in an instant. It is a thought on the verge, marveled before an instantaneous reality, surprised by truth. The awareness he managed to turn into a locus of praise and "wonder of being" is none other than the awareness of a threshold.

In *Siloë,* Gaston Roupnel's proposed meditation of time, Bachelard seizes on this revelation of a threshold that forever reappears and begins again. A threshold one leaves and reencounters, ceaselessly. The friendship he felt toward the companion of his Burgundian promenades, the complicity with his intuitions, justifies what one might call a method of sympathy. Bachelard turns friendship into an experience of discovery, into a mode of analysis. He does not explain . . . Could poetry be explained? "An intuition cannot be proven; it is experienced" [*L'intuition de l'instant,*

This translation features a selection from Lescure's "Introduction à la poétique de Bachelard" (Éditions Denoël, 1966), published in Gaston Bachelard's *L'intuition de l'instant* (Paris: Stock, 1992), 137–49. Notes to this text and references to works cited have been supplied by the translator. Unless otherwise noted, passages quoted from Bachelard's works are all translated by me (E.R.P.). Page numbers refer to the French editions of Bachelard's texts.

8].[1] Instead he chooses to elaborate on the implications of Roupnel's thought, displaying his own thought process in response to a book whose beauties offer themselves, in turn, as secret clues to friendship. Everything in *Siloë* teaches him the way to proceed. Yet more than a guide to thinking, it is a guide to life that he seeks. Or rather, since living is thinking, it is by living his thought that he finds the way of thinking his life.

"We have therefore taken the intuitions of *Siloë* back as close as possible to their source, as we strive to heed the promptings that these intuitions could provide to philosophical meditation" [*Intuition*, 8]. This act of reviving the thought of a friend in one's own thought, which one must live henceforth, this way of reinitiating moments of past consciousness (apparently immobilized in a book) to give them a future, this self-animation which is also the reanimation of another, adds exalted affection and gratitude to the pleasure of life. The reclusive life of study discovers itself in communion with another being made suddenly real. The solitude to which the instant ceaselessly remits us, finds itself repeatedly broken by the progress of the mind that at every step carries the step that carries it along, propelling the real presence that impels it. Bachelard's generous spirit hoped that solitary readers would thus discover and recognize the fraternal joy proposed by genuine thought.

I could not envision or suggest a better method for those preparing to read Bachelard's own *L'intuition de l'instant* (1932). If one expects to find a system within his work, one should be suspicious of the man who professed the end of an era of great systems. A metaphysician he was, no doubt; and his work is indeed a metaphysics of being, but one that paves the way to living research more than to knowledge per se—to a mode of questioning more than to an answer. It retains the necessary pinch of possibility within the coherence of rational thought, so that it may not be enclosed within a scholarly definition where the clearest reason at times lets itself be undone.

Bachelard's thought traces its lines in the manner of hints rather than hard rules. We readers need to convince ourselves that—as the preface to his *Psychanalyse du feu* (1938) will later suggest—we will not accrue knowledge or accumulate perishable information in reading these works. Instead, we will heighten our power to live, sharpen the art of conducting an intellectual life, and learn not to take ourselves too seriously.

Readers will encounter in Bachelard's work a biography of wonderstruck wisdom. They will discover an exemplary path where the domains of solitude and courage, silence and speech, reverie and reality, all become available to the will that yearns to refine the human heart and awaken its spirit of friendship.

It is a matter of virtue. I would invite readers to abandon here any academic ideas about what it means to be a philosopher. In evoking Bachelard, we must instead imagine a wise man whose ambition is to vouch for this life—both for his sake and that of others. The inter-subjectivity of dreams leads him to a shared world. He devotes himself to leading his existence beyond the everyday agitations that consume the soul. Beyond the transgressions of passion that lead us astray. He aspires to raise himself to those moments of intensity from which one might develop a philosophy of repose.

Bachelard no doubt reached the goal he had ultimately set for himself from the outset of *La dialectique de la durée*. Though not without irony: "A philosophy of repose is not a philosophy of complete repose."[2]

The doctor who assisted at his deathbed said: "I come from seeing a soul that for the last twenty years had forgotten it had a body."

There is no natural human value. We are, and are not, of this world. This body, which belongs to the world, must be incorporated again and again into this world. What desperate means can come here to our aid? In fraternal fervor, two of the great departed fuse the injustice of their absence within my solitude. Both Paul Éluard and Gaston Bachelard equally understood that "to strengthen the heart, we need to reinforce passion with morality" [*Intuition*, 92]. Being human is a decision. Our values become inscribed as a result of the acts by which we ourselves fashion our time, from the instants we live.

Bent on perceiving no more than the ills generated in human psyches by former traumas, modern psychology is barely capable of discerning those aesthetic perspectives that deliver the advent of surprise in our hearts. Is it true that human beings are primarily moved by such ordinary needs? Doesn't the language by which we transform our impulses bear some reality within itself, something from the world it opens up for us? If we know the means by which our naive desires can be transformed into beautiful words, we forget that the beauty of those very words ultimately prevails over the needs we believed them to express, to the point of swaying them to commit their energies to different ends. To speak is not merely to translate a certain sense of malaise, but to enter the world of the word, where astonishing powers are at play.

A poet manages to imbue things with what partakes of their secret powers, releasing them to a reality they already carry within, however obscurely. As I ponder things in their given names, they come to awaken endless reveries in me, resonant word-forming reveries. Words ceaselessly offer to reveal novel realities within things. The ordinary singsongs of the heart are painfully inadequate. Reverie demands more. At each instant, the death of the instant forbids the poet from stopping, and hurls his history forth, toward a never-ending "and then." We are beings of the *over* and *beyond*. Whether we call ourselves surrealists or supernaturalists, it is always about the powers of a metamorphosis revealed by prefixes. All truly human conduct is meta-physical.

"A meditation on time is the preliminary task of every metaphysics" [*Intuition*, 3]. It is true that Bachelard's entire oeuvre is metaphysical. Hence to consider its core notion of imagination as a mere psychological faculty located somewhere between perception and memory would be to miss its point entirely.

The imagination is a specific faculty: "To it belongs that unreality function which is as psychically useful as the reality function" [*La terre et les rêveries de la volonté*, 3]. One could even read his later *Poétique de la rêverie* (1960) as a "critique of pure imagination" (after Kant), though Bachelard might have preferred labeling it "transcendental fantasy" (after Novalis). Often he would insist that "we must define human beings as the sum of those tendencies which impel us to surpass the human condition" [*L'eau et les rêves*, 23]. In the service of such tendencies, imagination deploys words. The world emerges therein. Citing Novalis, Bachelard claimed that "every single human faculty, every single act of the inner and outer worlds can be deduced from the productive imagination" [*La terre et les rêveries de la volonté*, 4–5].

The values of conversion, redemption, and purification exert a relentless attraction over this metaphysical soul. The term "pure" recurs ceaselessly in Bachelard's works: as "pure consciousness" in *Dialectique de la durée;* as a "pure instant," "pure beginning," and "pure act" in *Lautréamont;* as "pure spontaneity" in his "Poétique du Phénix."[3]

Appearing with such frequency, this attribute deserves to undergo a substantial mutation within our understanding. We need to rethink the notion of purity—purity as a factor of reality. In the nomenclature of objective elements to be detached from the confused world where language operates, purity must be considered as a proof of being—even as its motor, its energy source. When speaking of mathematics, Bachelard praises "the joy of living a non-life in the abstract"—the implication being that there is an impure life that fails to attain being. If it is necessary to "remove oneself from the obligations of desire," to "break the parallelism of will and happiness," this means that every thing can and must suffer a metamorphosis in order to be [*Lautréamont*, 52]. Non-life is neither an elsewhere nor an "anywhere out of the world." Being equal to life, its apparent absence is but a matter of naïveté. For it is the very here-and-now, transformed. "The main function of poetry is to transform us." And "it is the prerogative of certain poets to live in a state of permanent metamorphosis." That is why "the beautiful cannot be reproduced; it must be produced. It borrows from life elementary energies which are first of all transformed, then transfigured" [*Lautréamont*, 60].

Mathematician and poet converge. Lautréamont's mathematical soul "remembered those hours when he managed to arrest his impulses, when he annihilated life within himself in order to think, when he loved abstraction as a beautiful solitude." And it is in Paul Éluard that Bachelard finds the proof of "a soul for whom expression is more than life" [*Lautréamont*, 55].

It is life itself, and only life, that can be more than life. Verbalized life.[4] Language is a mode of existence. It is in language that discovery takes place. It does not reproduce the world; it produces it. That which it bears does not exist outside itself or before itself. It is not added to life; it adds to life. And it is life and always life which, in language, is added to life.

Even when turned toward the past, the word is faced with a "not yet," forced to admit an absence where it reencounters the future. "Reveries towards childhood do not consist in remembering . . . Bachelard's entire poetics rebels against such false realism," François Dagognet writes in a splendid book devoted to his friend and teacher.

Bachelard admired this former student of his. They too, no doubt, held each other in "modest sympathy."[5] His passion for teaching was yet another form of that unique gift for friendship he had. One could not but reciprocate and share such friendship. More than a feeling, it was an awareness of values.

François Dagognet notes that, from *La poétique de l'espace* onward, Bachelard blends his own reveries with the images of poets on which he bases his reflections. One might think he is remembering, turning back, renouncing the future for the morose complacencies of a past he indulges in recapitulating. Not quite, however, for in this past he discovers the future. "Objective and dated memory with all its events is, for Bachelard, but a way in which human beings manage to deceive themselves and others—no more than a minor legend invented by adults. Beyond its well-placed "facts," a real and permanent childhood lives on in us—a childhood that emerges only belatedly in old age, when the noises of existence begin to fade away . . . Bachelard performs bold inversions: childhood becomes a future that is forever beginning, a continual creation. . . "[6]

One certainly finds in these works memories of Bachelard's own childhood. From them, perhaps, readers will someday extract a "history of reveries" that might read:

I was born in a region of rivers and rivulets, in an area of Champagne—the Vallage, so named because of its countless valleys. The most beautiful of dwellings, for me, would be embedded within a little valley on the shore of living waters, under the brief shadows of weeping willows and reeds. And when October comes with its mists over the river. . .

When I was ill, my father used to light the fire in my bedroom. Carefully he would prop the logs over the kindling . . . slipping in a handful of wood shavings between the firedogs . . .

From the teeth of the chimney hook he would hang a black cauldron. The tripod casserole fit right into the burning ashes. Blowing mightily into the iron pipe, my grandmother would reawaken the sleeping flames . . .

For the great winter feasts, during my childhood, we used to make sugar lumps flambéed with brandy. My father would pour grape marcs from our vineyard into a large dish. In the middle, he would place morsels of broken sugar, the very largest from our sugar bowl. From the moment the lit match touched the tip of a sugar cube, the blue flame would descend with a crackling noise toward the spreading alcohol. My mother would snuff out the excess heat. That was the hour of mystery and solemn feasting in a minor key . . .

A well left a mark on my early childhood. I'd never come near it except when led by the hand of a grandfather. Who was afraid: the grandfather or the child? . . .

Yet such memories should be read as those of a future, as a childhood to be shaped, as an awaited poetry. One cannot stop living, always gaining life upon life. To arrest one's past would be no more than to become trapped in one's past. The dramas one finds therein would amount to mere representations. They might satisfy a romantic complacency to think of oneself (or the desire for others to think of one) as a center of captivating tragedies. But what they would define would be no more than a fictional character. Not the type of person Bachelard envisioned radiantly alive.

Accustomed to mocking himself, toward his middle years Bachelard learned to give his assent not to what he was, but to what he needed to be, in order to be. Along with work, living itself is a moral act. A metaphysical morality is born of *L'intuition de l'instant.* "For the man who spiritualizes his emotions," Bachelard would write just a few years later, "the resulting purification is of a strange sweetness, and the consciousness of purity pours forth a strange light" [*Psychanalyse du feu,* 172].[7]

The paths toward purification presuppose the possibility of reiterated births. They call for the instant to shatter temporal fate, for discontinuity to authorize surprising advents. If "the cruelest mourning is the consciousness of a future betrayed," the obstinate evidence of time as purveyor of wonder, surprise, and novelty is indeed associated with this initial revelation of suffering, with this irruption of the plundering instant. That which thrusts me into the jaws of death is also that which offers me the chance to be reborn.

For never—not for a single moment—are we the sum of our past. Each instant discovered is what grants new sense, at every instant, to the senseless history we have lived so far. It is what grants our effort some of the meaning we need in order to seize the soul that shall be ours.

A modicum of happiness is possible in this world. Even when its presence is realized through an absence forever thrust upon us:

> . . . *the purest happiness, the one we have lost.*[8]

It may well be that happiness, in order to be, must first be lost. We human beings are the vast energy of our transmutation. In this way, we are our own future till death. Our freedom surely consists in this. Our words bind us, in our reverie, to our future. They are not the expression of "previous thought." They are the very birth of thought. Far from being slaves to our past, of being enchained by our remorse and tied to our fears, we embody the freedom to be what we are not. In order to draw out from its absence that being which is always to come, we need a poetics. Extreme darkness, that pure unknown that awaits our illumination while it illumines us with its destruction, grants us our secret figure. Not *still* but *forever* secret. Our figure of the secret. We are the animal who by itself assigns to itself its endless discovery. In Bachelard's work, novelty is a factor of reality. Therein poetry is designated as "one of the forms of human audacity."

For a spirit enamored of knowing and living, all knowledge is essentially inadequate, and all life is found wanting. "What Siloam . . . will allow us to understand the supreme *order* of things? What divine grace will grant us the power to harmonize the beginnings of being and the beginnings of thought?" [*Intuition,* 5]. There is a path of science and a path of poetry. Without ever having insisted on reconciling his diurnal and nocturnal powers, Bachelard noted that a human being—whether scientist or poet—is not a given. A human being is *made.* As in poetry, "all real progress in scientific thinking calls for a conversion."[9]

It is in terms of progression that we must read a philosopher such as Bachelard for whom beauty evolves in the work of poets and artists—i.e., for whom there is progress in art, *hence* progress in life. Experiencing his exaltation, we must follow him. "Poetry is wonderment precisely at word-level—in the word, by the word" [*La flamme d'une chandelle,* 77].

Only by choosing death can one escape death. Not the death of absolute being, but the death of human time which acts upon time and tears it apart—that death whose irruption into our existence makes life's emergence possible; that void into which we fling our will; that absence toward which we unceasingly commit our freedom for the sake of unforeseen births.

At that point, a human being is equal to world, indeed its contemporary, delivered along with things. What the instant offers is truly "a being and objects, all at once."[10] At the world's edge, we and the world hesitate with the same hesitation. On the verge of being, within the instant of an instant, I am not yet that which is annihilated. Existing within the instant of an emergence, of an invasion of silence, I do not feel abandoned to a past that swallows me up. Because it is always something to be conquered, true life is present. It is at work in every one of our waking moments. It is contemporaneous with our words. Like a bird of fire, it is reborn—it invites us to be reborn from our ashes. It is not enough to say that for us a new life is possible. We must affirm that it is our "human destiny." Bachelard establishes his philosophy with a wink and a smile. Perhaps a new life is quite simply life renewed—life forever, and at every single moment, new.

Having gone through a "Psychoanalysis of Fire," the lifework of this wise teacher was bound to end with a "Poetics of the Phoenix." Now, looking back on his remarkable philosophical itinerary, it makes sense that the first work to engage his readers in a metamorphosis of purity should have been an "Intuition of the Instant."

A Short Biography of Gaston Bachelard

Gaston Bachelard was born on June 27, 1884, at Bar-sur-Aube, Champagne, where his parents ran a tobacco and newspaper store. He spent his early years in that city. After obtaining his *baccalauréat* in 1903, he became a postal clerk at Remineront. In 1906 he began military service as a telegraphist in the Twelfth Dragoons at Pont-à-Mousson until 1913. On leave of absence to further his studies, he prepared for the examination for engineering students in telegraphy, while earning a *licence* in mathematical science from the Lycée Saint-Louis. On July 8, 1914, he married a schoolteacher from his region. That same summer, he was mobilized to fight in World War I. He served thirty-eight months in the trenches, earning the Croix de Guerre.

After the war, in 1919, Bachelard's life took a decisive turn as he began his teaching career, initially as professor of physics and chemistry at the Collège de Bar-sur-Aube. On June 20, 1920, his wife died, leaving him a daughter, Suzanne Bachelard, who would years later become a well-known Husserl scholar in her own right. It is at this time that Gaston Bachelard started his studies in philosophy, obtaining first his *licence* and then his *agrégation* in 1922, after which he continued teaching at Bar-sur-Aube, as professor of philosophy and science.

In 1927, Bachelard earned his doctorate in letters at the Sorbonne, defending two theses: *Essai sur la connaissance approchée,* and *Étude sur l'évolution d'un problème de physique: La propagation thermique dans les solides* (yet to be translated into English). These two works would become a prelude to numerous publications—among which the best known are now those devoted to the elemental or material imagination (fire, water, air, earth), currently available in English through the Bachelard Translation Series of the Dallas Institute Publications, directed by Joanne Stroud.

In 1930 Bachelard became professor of philosophy at the University of Dijon, where he taught until 1940, at which time he was named chair of the history and philosophy of science at the Sorbonne (1940–54), where he succeeded Abel Rey. Throughout these years he actively participated in fermenting intellectual and artistic circles in Paris, collaborating in works by Jean Wahl, Marc Chagall, Henri de Waroquier,

Albert Flocon, and others, while also serving as director of the Institute of the History of Science.

Bachelard continued to publish in the fields of scientific epistemology and the poetic imagination, following this dual philosophical and pedagogical track, until the end his career. In 1951 he was promoted to the rank of *officier* in the Legion of Honor. In 1954 he retired from the Sorbonne, and was appointed honorary professor for an additional academic year (1954–55). In 1960 he was raised to the rank of *commandeur* in the Legion of Honor, and received the "Grand Prix National des Lettres" in 1961 for the publication of his *Poetics of Space* (*La poétique de l'espace*, 1957). On October 16, 1962, he died in Paris, survived by his daughter Suzanne, who passed away in 2008.

Notes

Bracketed notes are the translator's.

Introduction

1. Ernest Renan, *Souvenirs d'enfance et de jeunesse* (Paris: Calmann-Lévy, 1947), Préface, iii.
2. *Life and Habit* (London: A.C. Fifield, 1910). [Bachelard cites from Valéry Larbaud's French translation, *La vie et l'habitude* (Paris: La Nouvelle Revue, 1922): "Si une verité n'est pas assez solide pour supporter qu'on la dénature et qu'on la malmène, elle n'est pas d'une espèce bien robuste" (17). Larbaud's French sentence has been retranslated here into English to highlight the metaphor of truth as "a living species" Bachelard picks up on, even though that metaphor is only implicit in Butler's original English: "Unless a matter be true enough to stand a good deal of misrepresentation, its truth is not of a very robust order" (*Life and Habit*, 1).]

Chapter 1

1. Gaston Roupnel, *Siloë* (Paris: Librairie Stock, 1927), 108. [Hereafter cited as *Siloë*; translations are mine.—E.R.P.]
2. [See Roch C. Smith, "Gaston Bachelard and Critical Discourse: The Philosopher of Science as Reader." *Stanford French Review* 5 (1981): 217–28.]
3. [Roupnel's term for this form of temporal rupture and renewal is *assaillante* (>Lat. *as + salire*, to leap), i.e., "peppered with striking leaps that punctuate the flow of life," hence my rendering it as a "pulsating form."]
4. [Echoes of Novalis's doctrine of *Zufallsregel*—the "rule of accident" or "chance"—can be sensed in this Roupnelian thesis. See Kristin Pfefferkorn, *Novalis* (New Haven, Conn.: Yale University Press, 1988), 30ff. In his final years, Bachelard confessed to having become a fervent reader of Novalis (*The Flame of a Candle* [Dallas: Dallas Institute, 1988], 14).]
5. See also Bergson, *Essai sur les données immédiates de la conscience* (Paris: Félix Alcan, 1912), 82. [Trans. by F. L. Pogson as *Time and Free Will: An Essay on the Immediate Data of Consciousness* (c. 1910; New York: Harper and Row, 1960), chapter 2; henceforth cited as *Time and Free Will*.]

6. [Bachelard is referring to one of the most important failed experiments in the history of physics—often described as "the kicking-off point for the theoretical aspects of the Second Scientific Revolution"—performed by Albert Michelson and Edward Morley, in 1887, at what is now Case Western Reserve University.]

7. [This is a general reference to the philosophy of Baruch Spinoza (1632–1677). In particular, see his *Ethics*, trans. Andrew Boyle, revised by G. H. R. Parkinson (London: Dent, 1989).]

8. From a more psychological viewpoint than ours, Jean Marie Guyau had written in *La genèse de l'idée du temps:* "The idea of time . . . can be traced back to a perspectival effect" (1890; Paris: L'Harmattan, 1998), ii. [All translations of this text (hereafter cited as *Genèse*) are mine.]

9. See Maurice Halbwachs, *Les cadres sociaux de la mémoire* (Paris: Alcan, 1925, 1935).

10. [These lines from Bachelard's original 1932 text were unfortunately omitted in the 1992 edition of *L'intuition de l'instant:* "[tel souvenir intime] où nous avons joué le destin de notre coeur. Mais si la localisation des souvenirs est si nettement indirecte, si elle doit, pour être précise, multiplier ses références aux domains les plus écartés de notre vie intime" (35). I have restored them in this translation for their key value in illustrating Bachelard's point.]

11. [The French wordplay between *l'attention* (attention) and *l'attente* (waiting)—including the verb *attendre* (to wait) further below—needs to be highlighted since it does not carry over as such into English.]

12. [In Bacon's precise words: "But it is the empty things that are vast; things solid are most contracted, and lie in little room" (Preface, *The Instauratio magna* [*The Great Instauration*], 1620; printed in http://www.constitution.org/bacon /instauration.htm).]

13. [Eternity is here understood as "infinity" (compare Couturat's *infini mathématique*).]

14. [This well-known line, "donner un sens plus pur aux mots de la tribu," is quoted from Mallarmé's sonnet "Le tombeau d'Edgar Poe."]

15. [French logician and philosopher Louis Couturat (1868–1914) is particularly known for his writings on Leibniz's logic and on the foundations of mathematics. Bachelard had discussed Couturat's *De l'infini mathématique*, with its theory of fractions, in his earlier *Essai sur la connaissance approchée* (Paris, 1928).]

16. [Bachelard considers each instant to be a bearer of rich possibilities—some of which become realized in an actual phenomenon, yet many of which remain hovering as an aura of conditionals. The phenomenon as "denominator" is thus intuited in its profuse potentiality—encompassing what *might* become its contingent manifestation at some point, even though such potentiality is indeterminate, and hence cannot be clearly grasped.]

17. [The "measuring instrument" referred to here is *l'esprit* (mind/spirit)—a faculty of attunement, intuition, and knowledge assumed by Bachelard to be at least as subtle as any phenomenon given it to assess. It remains an open question whether Bachelard is here taking into consideration what Jean-Luc Marion has recently coined "a saturated phenomenon" (after "the sublime" in Kant)—phenomenon which, by definition, surpasses the mind's capacity for clear and

precise apprehension, yet not necessarily its capacity for acknowledgment, acceptance, and appreciation. See also Marion, *The Visible and the Revealed*, trans. C. M. Gschwandtner et al. (New York: Fordham University Press, 2008), 18–48.]

18. [In his works on imagination, from *Psychoanalysis of Fire* (1938) to *Poetics of Reverie* (1960), Bachelard will explore such "illusion that precedes thought" under the rubric of "reverie."]

19. [Jean de La Fontaine (1621–1695), one of the great seventeenth-century poets, is best known for his *Fables*.]

20. [This passage, as well as Bachelard's allusion in the previous paragraph to "ceaselessly recovered illusions" which are "no longer pure illusions," remits us to Proust's masterpiece *Remembrance of Things Past*, trans. C.K. Scott Moncrieff and Terence Kilmartin (New York: Random House, 1981).]

21. [*Anisotropy* is a scientific term denoting the heterogeneity of physical properties with respect to varying directions.]

22. [This point in Guyau's posthumously published *Genèse de l'idée de temps* (1890) anticipates Husserl's notion of "protention" in his lectures on time, delivered around the turn of the century. See *On the Phenomenology of the Consciousness of Internal Time (1893–1917)*, trans. John B. Brough (Boston: Kluwer Academic, 1991), §14, §40, and 144f.]

23. Henri Bergson, *Essai sur les données immédiates de la conscience*, 117. [Bachelard is referring to the section in chapter 3 where Bergson discusses physical determinism, differentiating this from the "realm of life": in the latter he claims, "duration does seem to act like a cause" (see *Time and Free Will*, 153).]

Chapter 2

1. [Bachelard's thesis, here, is that a habit cannot be explained as an "efficient cause"—i.e., as the direct effect of the past upon the present. See also Aristotle's "four causes" (efficient, material, formal, final) postulated as guiding nature's creative processes in his *Physics*, book 2, chapter 3, 194b-195a. Bachelard will tacitly reinterpret each of these Aristotelian "causes" in the argument that follows, elaborating on them even further in his subsequent books on the elemental imagination.]

2. Koyré, *La philosophie de Jacob Boehme* (Paris: J. Vrin, 1929), 131. [Best known as a philosopher of science, Alexandre Koyré (1892–1964) started out as a historian of religion. Much of his originality for the period rests on his ability to ground his studies of modern science on the history of religion and metaphysics. His well-known *From the Closed World to the Infinite Universe* (Baltimore: Johns Hopkins University Press, 1957) provides a summation of his philosophical outlook.]

3. [See Aristotle's account of the "formal cause" (aesthetic action as *eidos* or *ratio*) in nature's generative processes, via analogy with human creation (*Physics*, book 2, chapter 3, 194b-195a).]

4. *Life and Habit*, 155; *La vie et l'habitude*, 149. [Samuel Butler (1835–1902) set out, in this book, to offer his own ideas about evolution, which he believed would supplement Darwin's work. Butler contended that inheritance was partly

based on the fact that *habit* ingrains certain features in our genes so that they can be transmitted to later generations. He felt he was adding something important to Darwin, since the idea of "use-inheritance" had been part of Darwin's original theory, where he could not account for variations by natural selection. By the time *Life and Habit* appeared in 1878, however, it had turned into a fierce attack on Darwin's theory. Ultimately Butler objected to what he regarded as Darwin's exclusion of Mind from the universe. He wanted to reinstate a model where individuals had some modicum of control over what *form* they took, as a consequence of their *actions*. See http://www.victorianweb.org/science/butler.html.]

5. See *Life and Habit*, 156. [*La vie et l'habitude*, 150, 151.]

6. [This is a Bachelardian interpretation of Aristotle's "material cause" (*Physics*, book 2, chapter 3, 194b)—a necessary though not sufficient factor in both natural and artistic production—conceived here in terms of the generation of living beings.]

7. *Life and Habit*, 130. [*La vie et l'habitude*, 128.]

8. [In geometry, to *exscribe* means to draw a circle outside a triangle so that it touches one side and the lines obtained by producing the other two sides.]

9. [Bachelard's remark here anticipates the postmodern theory of "the circle of looking glasses"—the interplay of self-multiplying mirror images without depth or interiority—later to become a recurring concern of twentieth-century thinkers such as Jacques Derrida and Roland Barthes. See Richard Kearney, *Poetics of Imagining* (New York: Fordham University Press, 1998),178ff.]

10. [The finalistic element in this passage harks back to the Aristotelian notion of a "final cause" (*Physics*, book 2, chapter 3, 195a), here illustrated by Bachelard (after Roupnel) in terms of the development of living beings.]

11. ["Finalism" is the theory that *natural processes* (not only human productions) can be explained in terms of their ends, purposes, final causes. In *Creative Evolution*, Bergson relates "finalism" to the "doctrine of teleology," critiquing Leibniz's version as an "inverted mechanism" whereby *all is given* and "beings merely realize a program previously arranged"—the difference being that finalism "holds in front of us the light with which it claims to guide us, instead of putting it behind. It substitutes the attraction of the future for the impulsion of the past" (*Creative Evolution*, trans. Arthur Mitchell [New York: Courier Dover, 1998], 39).]

12. Henri Bergson, *Matière et mémoire* (Paris: F. Alcan, 1896), 231. [Bergson, *Matter and Memory*, trans. Nancy Margaret Paul and W. Scott Palmer (New York: Zone Books, 1988), 207; translation slightly amended.]

Chapter 3

1. [Bachelard is alluding here to the power of intentionality—the fundamental "habit of being" mentioned in chapter 2 as underlying all others. Although this general habit tends to sink beneath the threshold of consciousness, for Bachelard it still remains a function of human will, forever exposed to its sanction.]

2. See Henri Bergson, *Durée et simultanéité* (Paris: Presses Universitaires de France, 1922), 70. [English trans. by Leon Jacobson, *Duration and Simultaneity*, ed. by Robin Durie (Manchester, Eng.: Clinamen, 1999), 30ff.]

3. [The French noun *réciproque* is a mathematical term (Eng. noun, "reciprocal") which means "a function or expression so related to another that their product is unity; an inverse."]

4. [A prolific novelist, dramatist, and critic, Octave Mirbeau (1848–1917) is best known today for his play, *Les affaires sont les affaires* (Paris: Fasquelle, 1924). Bachelard provides no specific reference for this comment.]

5. Henri Bergson, *Durée et simultanéité*, 42. [Here Bachelard slightly misquotes Bergson's phrase "multiplicity without divisibility" (compare *Duration and Simultaneity*, 30).]

6. [What is refuted in *Siloë* is the notion of a permanent, immutable substance. The trinity proposed in *Siloë* is "phenomenal," rather than "ontological," as Bachelard proceeds to clarify.]

7. [Besides Bergson's theses on time, Bachelard is most likely alluding here to Martin Heidegger's existential analysis of "temporality and care" in *Being and Time* (*Sein und Zeit*, 1927), division 2, sec. 3. See also Husserl's *On the Phenomenology of the Consciousness of Internal Time (1893–1917).*]

8. [Personal communication from Gaston Roupnel, author of *Siloë* and Bachelard's close friend at the University of Dijon in the late 1920s and 1930s.]

Conclusion

1. [Jean Guéhenno (1890–1978) was a French literary critic, writer, and humanist. His *Caliban parle* (Paris: Bernard Grasset, 1928) is an "autobiographic" account of Caliban himself contesting philosopher Ernest Renan's earlier account (*Caliban*, 1878).]

2. [Bachelard will further elaborate on this allusion to the "smiling regret"—a key insight in Baudelaire's "Recueillement" (*Les fleurs du mal*, 1868)— in his follow-up essay, "Poetic Instant and Metaphysical Instant" (see Appendix A, note 4, below).]

Appendix A

1. [The notion of *order* (>Lat. *ordos* = rank, degree) here presupposes the idea of hierarchical *valuation*, which Bachelard develops below.]

2. Charles Baudelaire, *Petits poèmes en prose* (*Le Spleen de Paris*) (Paris: Corti, 1969). The French *heure* has been translated alternately, in this case, as "time" (telling time) and "hour" (to allude to the fullness of time evoked by the round images of a clock's face and a cat's fathomless eye). Compare with Edward K. Kaplan's translation of Baudelaire's "The Clock" in *The Parisian Prowler*, 34.

3. Compare Baudelaire's *The Flowers of Evil* (*Les fleurs du mal*). See note 4, below.

4. [Charles Baudelaire, "Recueillement," in *Les fleurs du mal* (1868; Édition du Centenaire, 1957), 254–55. See the "Selected Bibliography" for further bibliographical details.]

5. Baudelaire, *Mon coeur mis à nu* (Geneva: Librairie Droz, 2001), no. 72, xl.

6. [Bachelard sheds light on the ethical significance of "the instant of the human person" in his preface to Martin Buber's *Je et tu* (*I and Thou*), trans. Geneviève Bianquis (Paris: Aubier Montaigne, 1938), 7–15. See Edward K. Kaplan's translation of Bachelard's 1938 preface along with his accompanying philosophical analysis, "Imagination and Ethics: Gaston Bachelard and Martin Buber," in *International Studies in Philosophy* 35, no. 1 (2003): 75–88.]

Appendix B

1. Henceforth abbreviated as *Intuition*.

2. Gaston Bachelard, *La dialectique de la durée* (Paris: Boivin, 1936), 1.

3. Published posthumously as part of *Fragments d'une poétique du feu* (Paris: Presses Universitaires de France, 1988), 5–24, 61–104.

4. Bachelard would grant primacy to the *élan vocal* over the élan vital, in contradistinction with Bergson. See Jean-François Perraudin, "A Non-Bergsonian Bachelard," in *Continental Philosophy Review* 41 (2008), 463–79.

5. Bachelard had described his friendship with Gaston Roupnel as marked by "a modest sympathy" (see *Intuition*, 136).

6. Citation not provided.

7. This line was translated by Alan Ross, *Psychoanalysis of Fire* (Boston: Beacon, 1964), 101.

8. *Intuition*, 92.

9. See *Lautréamont*, 155–156. See also *Psychanalyse du feu*, 11; *Formation de l'esprit scientifique* (1938; Paris: Vrin, 1999), 15–16.

10. "Instant poétique et instant métaphysique" (*Intuition*, 103).

Selected Bibliography

This bibliography is presented in three sections: (1) works by Gaston Bachelard; (2) works and authors cited by Bachelard in *Intuition of the Instant* and in "Poetic Instant and Metaphysical Instant"; and (3) works cited in the translator's notes.

Works by Gaston Bachelard

Essai sur la connaissance approchée (1928). Paris: Vrin, 1969.

Etude sur l'évolution d'un problème de physique: La propagation thermique dans les Solides. Paris: Vrin 1928.

Valeur inductive de la relativité. Paris: Vrin, 1929.

Le pluralisme cohérent de la chimie moderne. Paris: Vrin, 1932.

L'intuition de l'instant (1932). Paris: Éditions Stock, 1992.

Les intuitions atomistiques. Paris: Boivin, 1933.

Le nouvel esprit scientifique. Paris: Alcan, 1934. [*The New Scientific Spirit.* Trans. Arthur Goldhammer. Boston: Beacon, 1984.]

La dialectique de la durée (1936). Paris: Presses Universitaires de France, 1950. [*The Dialectic of Duration.* Trans. Mary McAllester Jones. Manchester, Eng.: Clinamen, 2000.]

Formation de l'esprit scientifique (1938). Paris: Vrin, 1999. [*Formation of the Scientific Mind.* Trans. Mary McAllester Jones. Manchester, Eng.: Clinamen, 2002.]

Préface à Martin Buber, *Je et tu.* Trans. from German by Geneviève Bianquis. Paris: Aubier Montaigne, 1938 (7–15). [Preface to Martin Buber's *I and Thou.* Trans. Edward K. Kaplan. In *International Studies in Philosophy* 35, no. 1 (2003): 89–94.]

La psychanalyse du feu. Paris: Librairie Gallimard, 1938. [*Psychoanalysis of Fire.* Trans. Alan C. M. Ross. Boston: Beacon, 1964.]

Lautréamont. Paris: Librairie José Corti, 1939. [*Lautréamont.* Trans. Robert Scott Dupree. Dallas: Dallas Institute, 1986.]

Philosophie du non. Paris: Presses Universitaires de France, 1940. [*Philosophy of No.* Trans. G. C. Waterston. New York: Orion, 1968.]

L'eau et les rêves. Paris : Librairie José Corti, 1942. [*Water and Dreams.* Trans. Edith Farrell. Dallas: Pegasus Foundation, 1983.]

L'air et les songes. Paris: Librairie José Corti, 1943. [*Air and Dreams.* Trans. Edith R. and C. Frederick Farrell. Dallas: Dallas Institute, 1988.]

La terre et les rêveries de la volonté. Paris: José Corti, 1947. [*Earth and Reveries of Will*. Trans. Kenneth Haltman. Dallas: Dallas Institute, 2002.]

La terre et les rêveries du repos. Paris : José Corti, 1948. [*Earth and Reveries of Repose*. Trans. Mary McAllester Jones. Dallas: Dallas Institute, 2011.]

Le rationalisme appliquée. Paris: Presses Universitaires de France, 1949.

L'activité rationaliste de la physique contemporaine. Paris: Presses Universitaires de France, 1951.

Le matérialisme rationnel. Paris: Presses Universitaires de France, 1953.

La poétique de l'espace. Paris: Presses Universitaires de France, 1958. [*Poetics of Space*. Trans. Maria Jolas. Boston: Beacon, 1969.]

La poétique de la rêverie. Paris: Presses Universitaires de France, 1960. [*Poetics of Reverie*. Trans. Daniel Russell. Boston: Beacon, 1969.]

La flamme d'une chandelle. Paris: Presses Universitaires de France, 1961. [*The Flame of a Candle*. Trans. Joni Caldwell. Dallas: Dallas Institute, 1988.]

Fragments d'une poétique du feu. Paris: Presses Universitaires de France, 1988. [*Fragments of a Poetics of Fire*. Trans. Kenneth Haltman. Dallas: Dallas Institute, 1990.]

Works and Authors Cited by Bachelard

Baudelaire, Charles. *Mon coeur mis à nu*. Geneva: Librairie Droz, 2001. [*My Heart Laid Bare and Other Prose Writings*. Trans. Norman Cameron. Ed. Peter Quennell. New York: Haskell House, 1975.]

———. *Petits poèmes en prose* (*Le Spleen de Paris*). Paris: Corti, 1969. [*The Parisian Prowler*. 2nd edition. Trans. Edward Kaplan. Athens: University of Georgia Press, 1997.]

———. "Recueillement." In *Les fleurs du mal*, Édition du Centenaire, 254–55. Paris: Jean-Jacques Pauvert, 1957. ["Meditation," in *The Flowers of Evil*. Trans. William Aggeler. Fresno, Calif.: Academy Library Guild, 1954.]

Bergson, Henri. *Durée et simultanéité: À propos de la théorie d'Einstein*. Paris: Félix Alcan, 1922, 1929. [*Duration and Simultaneity: Bergson and the Einsteinian Universe*. Trans. Leon Jacobson. Expanded edition, Robin Durie. Manchester, Eng.: Clinamen, 1999.]

———. *Essai sur les données immédiates de la conscience*. Paris: Félix Alcan, 1912. [*Time and Free Will: An Essay on the Immediate Data of Consciousness*. Trans. F. L. Pogson, c. 1910; New York: Harper and Row, 1960.]

———. *L'évolution créatrice*. Paris: Presses Universitaires de France, 1948 (first published in 1907). [*Creative Evolution*. Trans. Arthur Mitchell, 1911. New York: Dover, 1998.]

———. *Matière et mémoire*. Paris: F. Alcan, 1896. [*Matter and Memory*. Trans. Nancy Margaret Paul and W. Scott Palmer. New York: Zone Books, 1988.]

Butler, Samuel. "Life After Death." In *The Note-Books of Samuel Butler*. London: A.C. Fifield, 1918.

———. *Life and Habit*. London: A.C. Fifield, 1910. [*La vie et l'habitude*. French translation by Valéry Larbaud. Paris: La Nouvelle Revue, 1922.]

Guehénno, Jean. *Caliban parle.* Paris: Bernard Grasset, 1928.

Guyau, Jean-Marie. *La genèse de l'idée de temps.* Paris: Félix Alcan, 1890. Republished Paris: L'Harmattan, 1998.

Halbwachs, Maurice. *Les cadres sociaux de la mémoire.* Paris: 1925.

Koyré, Alexandre. *From the Closed World to the Infinite Universe.* Baltimore: John Hopkins University Press, 1957.

————. *La philosophie de Jacob Boehme.* Paris: J. Vrin, 1929.

Maeterlinck, Maurice. *Sagesse et destinée.* Paris: Bibliothèque-Charpentier, 1902.

Mallarmé, Stéphane. "Plusiers sonnets." In *Oeuvres complètes,* edited by Henri Mondor and G. Jean-Aubry, 67. Paris: Gallimard Pleiade, 1945.

————. *Selected Poems: Bilingual Edition.* Trans. Carlyle F. MacIntyre. Berkeley, Calif.: University of California Press, 2002.

Mirbeau, Octave. *Les affaires sont les affaires.* Paris: Fasquelle, 1924.

Renan, Ernest. *Souvenirs d'enfance et de jeunesse.* Paris: Calmann-Levy, 1947.

Roupnel, Gaston. *Siloë.* Paris: Librairie Stock, 1927.

Spinoza, Baruch. *Ethics.* Trans. Andrew Boyle, revised by G. H. R. Parkinson. London: Dent, 1989.

Works Cited in the Translator's Notes

Aristotle. *Physics,* Book 2. Trans. P. H. Wicksteed and F. M. Cornford. Loeb Classical Library. Cambridge, Mass.: Harvard University Press, 1980.

Heidegger, Martin. *Being and Time (Sein und Zeit,* 1927). Trans. John Macquarrie and Edward Robinson. New York: Harper and Row, 1962.

Husserl, Edmund. *On the Phenomenology of the Consciousness of Internal Time: 1893–1917* [*Vorlesungen zur Phänomenologie des innern Zeitbewusstseins,* 1928]. Trans. John Barnett Brough. Dordrecht: Kluwer Academic, 1991.

Kaplan, Edward. "Imagination and Ethics: Gaston Bachelard and Martin Buber." *International Studies in Philosophy* 35, no. 1 (2003): 75–88.

Kearney, Richard. *Poetics of Imagining.* New York: Fordham University Press, 1998.

Marion, Jean-Luc. *The Visible and the Revealed.* Trans. C. M. Gschwandtner et al. New York: Fordham University Press, 2008.

Perraudin, Jean-François. "Un Bachelard non-bergsonien." In *Gaston Bachelard: Du rêveur ironiste au pédagogue inspiré.* Edited by Jean Libis. Dijon: C.R.D.P., 1984 (61–76). ["A Non-Bergsonian Bachelard." Trans. Eileen Rizo-Patron. *Continental Philosophy Review* 41 (2008): 463–79.]

Pfefferkorn, Kristin. *Novalis: A Romantic's Theory of Language and Poetry.* New Haven, Conn.: Yale University Press, 1988.

Proust, Marcel. *Remembrance of Things Past* [*Recherche du temps perdu,* 1913–27]. Trans. C. K. Scott Moncrieff and Terence Kilmartin. New York: Random House, 1981.

Smith, Roch C. "Gaston Bachelard and Critical Discourse: The Philosopher of Science as Reader." *Stanford French Review* 5 (1981): 217–28.

Index

accident: of becoming, 15; of cultural growth, 10; doctrine of, 13, 14, 15, 75n4; of evolution, 13; external origin of, 14; individuals as sums of, 41; instant and, 10; Novalis on, 75n4; onslaught of, 10, 18; overlooked by Bergson, 13; as phenomenon of time, 19; as principle in Roupnel, 13. *See also* chance (*Zufallsregel*)

act: attention as, 11, 20; and becoming, 24; beginning, 13, 47; in Bergson's philosophy, 9, 13; and causality, 32; consciousness as, 12, 42, 56; creative, 10; as decision, 11, 12; habit as, 37, 43; hermeneutic, 65; of knowledge, 23; and instant, 30, 66; moral, 69; primordial, 37; of productive imagination, 67; pure, 67; of reason, 3; of rebirth as progress, 45; of redemptive synthesis, 56; revolutionary, 13; in Roupnel's philosophy, 11, 13, 24; and value, 66; of will, 11–12, 42, 45

action: after an act, 11–12; aesthetic or normative, 37, 77n3; in Bergson's philosophy, 11, 24; continuity vs. discontinuity of, 37; effective, 54; and evolution, 78n4; illusion of, 32; intimate, 24; nodes of, 15; repose and, 32; in Roupnel's philosophy, 13; simultaneous, 39; of time in Leibniz, 35

aesthetics, aesthetic: action, 37, 77n3; character, 4; coherence of being, 43, 46; conditions for continuity, 46, 54; imperative, 43; intuition, 55; perspectives, 66; progress, 48; turn in Bachelard's philosophy, xi

Althusser, Louis, ix

ambivalence: as synthesis of contraries, 56, 59, 60, 61, 62. *See also* instant

antithesis: as succession of contraries, 59

Aristotle: on causes, 77n1; on efficient cause, 77n1; on final cause, 78n10, on formal cause, 77n3; on material cause, 78n6, *Physics*, 77n1

arithmetic: arithmetization of time, 15, 22, 25; vs. geometric measure of time, 24, 31. *See also* atom, atomization of time

art: Bachelard's contribution to, ix–xi, 72–73; causality in, 77n3, 78n6; intellectual life as, 65; production, 78n6; progress in, 71; redemption by, 55; Roupnel on, 55, 56; summoning power of, 56. *See also* aesthetics/aesthetic

atom: as act/event, 13–15; and appearance of matter, 40; attention to being, 40; atomization of time, 15–16; becoming of, 35; chance and, 32; energy, 31, 32; and habit 40–41; indeterminate identity of, 41; and instant, 32, 40; and living cell, 27; as monad, 21; properties of, 21, 34; as pulse/frequency, 27, 31, 32; and quantum theory, 31; as radiation phenomenon, 27, 31–32; as reified instant, 18; spatial-temporal fusion in, 21; structural display of, 35; of time, 14–15; triple essence of, 21; virtual state of, 32

attention: act of, 11, 12, 20; to being, 40; as decision, 20; and duration, 20; ethics of, xii; habit and, 41; instantaneous, 11, 20; to life, 21; passionate, 7; as mental resumption/rebirth, 20; at point of space-time, 21; psychology of, 20; to uniform sensations, 49; and waiting, 20, 76n11; and will, 11, 20

Gaston Bachelard (1884–1962) began his teaching career in 1919 as professor of physics and chemistry at the Collège de Bar-sur-Aube. In 1927, Bachelard earned his doctorate in letters at the Sorbonne, specializing in epistemology. In 1930 he was appointed professor of philosophy at the University of Dijon, where he taught until 1940, at which time he was named chair of history and philosophy of science at the Sorbonne (1940–1954). In 1961 he won the French Grand Prix National des Lettres for his widely acclaimed *The Poetics of Space* (*La poétique de l'espace*, 1957).

Eileen Rizo-Patron holds a Ph.D. in Comparative Literature from Binghamton University, New York. She has published several articles on Gaston Bachelard, including "Awakening the Inner Ear: Gadamer and Bachelard in Search of a Living Logos," which addresses the hermeneutic wagers first proposed in *Intuition of the Instant*. With Richard Kearney she edited *Traversing the Heart: Journeys of the Inter-religious Imagination* (2010).

Lightning Source UK Ltd.
Milton Keynes UK
UKHW011822270123
416050UK00019B/367